"As President of the SNOC, I followed James' remarkable achievements not just on the field, but also their wider impact on sports in Singapore. His journey is an inspiration to a new generation of Singaporean athletes, as they seek to advance Singapore athletics on the world stage. James' life story, and particularly how he dealt with cancer, is a powerful reminder that the values we learn through sports, are equally applicable to many of life's toughest challenges."

Teo Chee Hean
Senior Minister and Coordinating Minister for National Security
Former President, Singapore National Olympic Council (1998–2014)

"Sports Excellence in 1993/94 was seeking heroes to champion our ambitious goals to win more medals at SEA and Asian Games. James Wong, our star sportsman then, became our role model for many years thereafter. He inspired countless young budding athletes in many sports through his discipline, dedication, determination and fighting spirit. Today, James remains true to form in his personal battle to fight against cancer. A great Singapore champion."

COL (Retired) Kwan Yue Yeong
Ex-Chief Executive Officer, Singapore Sports Council (1993–2004)

"James Wong has taken the brave step to share his cancer battle with others through this book which chronicles his cancer journey, inspiring hope to others who are battling cancer and paying tribute to the community that supported him alongside his sporting successes. He has reached out to the Singapore Cancer Society (SCS) offering to donate part of the proceeds from the sales of the book to support those impacted by cancer. SCS commends James for his bravery in sharing his cancer story and stepping forward to join SCS in the collective fight against cancer."

Albert Ching
Chief Executive Officer, Singapore Cancer Society

"I have known James since 1993. We were actually from the same school — Pasir Panjang Secondary School. Of course I was there in the 1950s, much earlier than him. James has really distinguished himself at the SEA Games winning nine discus gold medals across two-and-a-half decades. His name has become synonymous with the event locally and regionally! I am really looking forward to reading this book, especially knowing that it is written by Kenneth, a fellow athlete."

C. Kunalan
Former Vice-president, Singapore Athletics Association (2010–2016)

THE
LAST GOLD

James Wong: An Odyssey Through Sports and Cancer

THE LAST GOLD

James Wong: An Odyssey Through Sports and Cancer

Kenneth Khoo

World Scientific

NEW JERSEY · LONDON · SINGAPORE · BEIJING · SHANGHAI · HONG KONG · TAIPEI · CHENNAI · TOKYO

Published by

World Scientific Publishing Co. Pte. Ltd.
5 Toh Tuck Link, Singapore 596224
USA office: 27 Warren Street, Suite 401-402, Hackensack, NJ 07601
UK office: 57 Shelton Street, Covent Garden, London WC2H 9HE

National Library Board, Singapore Cataloguing in Publication Data
Name(s): Khoo, Kenneth (Educator).
Title: The last gold : James Wong : an odyssey through sports and cancer / Kenneth Khoo.
Description: Singapore : World Scientific Publishing Co. Pte. Ltd., [2025]
Identifier(s): ISBN 978-981-98-0011-7 (hardcover) | ISBN 978-981-98-0080-3 (paperback) |
    ISBN 978-981-98-0012-4 (ebook for institutions) |
    ISBN 978-981-98-0013-1 (ebook for individuals)
Subject(s): LCSH: Wong, James, 1969- | Bile ducts--Cancer--Patients--Singapore--Biography. |
    Track and field athletes--Singapore--Biography.
Classification: DDC 362.196994360092--dc23

British Library Cataloguing-in-Publication Data
A catalogue record for this book is available from the British Library.

Copyright © 2025 by World Scientific Publishing Co. Pte. Ltd.

All rights reserved. This book, or parts thereof, may not be reproduced in any form or by any means, electronic or mechanical, including photocopying, recording or any information storage and retrieval system now known or to be invented, without written permission from the publisher.

For photocopying of material in this volume, please pay a copying fee through the Copyright Clearance Center, Inc., 222 Rosewood Drive, Danvers, MA 01923, USA. In this case permission to photocopy is not required from the publisher.

For any available supplementary material, please visit
https://www.worldscientific.com/worldscibooks/10.1142/14023#t=suppl

Desk Editor: Jiang Yulin
Design and layout: Jimmy Low

Typeset by Stallion Press
Email: enquiries@stallionpress.com

*To the Cancer Warriors
and Their Caregivers,
May You Always Find Strength,
Courage and Fortitude
in the Darkest Hour.*

Contents

Foreword		x
Message by Professor Adrian Chiow		xii
Preface		xv

Part One	**Revelations**	
Chapter 1	"Why Me?"	3
Chapter 2	"This Seems Fun."	8
Chapter 3	The Killer Instinct	14
Chapter 4	The First of Many	20

Part Two	**The Hunt for Glory**	
Chapter 5	"Acceptance, then Adaptation."	27
Chapter 6	Close, But Still Not There Yet	35
Chapter 7	New System, New Adjustments	39
Chapter 8	The "Flop"	46
Chapter 9	A Shiny Piece of Metal	51

Part Three	**Onwards, to Victory**	
Chapter 10	"I've Done All I Can."	63
Chapter 11	The First Graduate in the Family	69
Chapter 12	*Willkommen, Herr* James Wong	74
Chapter 13	The Defending Champion	81
Chapter 14	The Aspiring Olympian	87
Chapter 15	The "Lord of the Ring"	91

Part Four	**The Tribe**	
Chapter 16	A Humbling Weakness	103
Chapter 17	The "Short Asian Man"	114
Chapter 18	Asia and the Commonwealth Beckon	120
Chapter 19	That Special "Feeling"	125
Chapter 20	Recriminations	136

Contents

Part Five	**Will He, Won't He?**	
Chapter 21	The Road to Recovery	147
Chapter 22	"Is He Even Human?"	153
Chapter 23	One Night in Kuala Lumpur	159
Chapter 24	A Lap of Honour	165
Chapter 25	The "Thrilla in Manila"	178
Part Six	**Setbacks…**	
Chapter 26	Not Again	189
Chapter 27	The Last Train to the Asiad	194
Chapter 28	"Thank You for Not Being There!"	198
Part Seven	**… and Comebacks**	
Chapter 29	The Last Push	204
Chapter 30	"8possible"	207
Chapter 31	The Other Side of the Fence	213
Chapter 32	"The Flag Bearer Must Win the Gold."	216
Part Eight	**The Last Gold**	
Chapter 33	History Beckons	227
Chapter 34	The Survivor	234
Chapter 35	A Final Word	238

James Wong's Career Highlights	244
James Wong's Cancer Timeline (2023)	251
Message from Singapore Cancer Society	254
Acknowledgements	255
Photo Credits	258
About the Author	260

Foreword

I first met James Wong in early 2000 when I was Vice-president of Training and Selection of the Singapore Athletics Association. To me, he was a titan, hurling his discus across the field aimed to smash records and make a name for himself on the international stage. His name was synonymous with victory, with Singapore.

This was a man who utterly dominated his regional rivals for a quarter of a century, setting an impressive standard for his teammates to follow. His victories held great significance as they stood out as a symbol of hope and belief to our athletes that they could compete with the best in the region and win.

But there was more to James Wong than the medals and records. There was a man beneath the athlete — a man of extraordinary resilience, determination, and heart. These qualities, I would later realise, were the bedrock of his success.

His dynamic confidence was a stabilising and reassuring factor for my management team. In our discussions about SEA Games gold medal projections, James was often the first name on our list.

Across my different presidential terms, James stood as a stalwart not only in his sporting achievements but also as a sports administrator where he provided invaluable support and advice in shaping the high-performance culture of Singapore athletics. His strong action management and single-minded determination to effect change enabled us to positively shape the tone and culture of the sport locally. His innate understanding of high performance and international networks proved invaluable in this regard.

The news of his cancer diagnosis was shocking to the community. Yet, even in the face of such adversity, James approached his battle with cancer with the same unwavering spirit that he had on the field.

In these pages, James shares his story with raw honesty and courage. It is a tale of triumph and tribulation, a testament to the human spirit. His journey, both on the field and in his fight against cancer, is a masterclass in perseverance.

Through his words, we witness the intricate tapestry of his life, where the athlete, the family man, and the cancer patient intertwine. It is a narrative that inspires, challenges, and ultimately, empowers. James' story is not just about him; it's a beacon of hope for everyone facing life's toughest battles.

I am privileged to write this foreword. It is a small token of my gratitude for the sportsmanship, the friendship, and the inspiration that James Wong has been to me.

Tang Weng Fei
Singaporean Athletics Association President
2004–2006, 2010–2016, 2018–2020

Message

When I first saw Mr. Wong Tuck Yim, there was little indication that this was a local track and field legend who was quietly sitting in the ward. This is testimony to his humility, that he did not tell a single soul who he was. In front of me was a concerned, well-spoken gentleman, perhaps just a little taller and bigger than usual, who took in information with a quiet thoughtfulness, even as I had to break the news of possible cancer.

It was only later in the clinic, after a short discussion with him and his wife, that he let on that he was "fairly active". At that moment, with likely a look of pure embarrassment, it suddenly dawned on me and I uttered, "Wait, you are James Wong? SEA Games discus…" and Jana, his wife, puts up 10 fingers for each of the 10 gold medals he won. There couldn't be a bigger hole I wished I could crawl into. Thus began a remarkable journey that I had the opportunity to witness and play a small part in.

Since recovering, James has been a support and friend to others who are on their own cancer journeys, taking time out to reassure and be with them and their families. His impact as an inspirational patient and champion advocate has been recognised at the 2024

Singapore Health Inspirational Patient and Caregiver Awards.

This book is a story about a man's battle with his cancer and his refusal to concede defeat. James brings us up close to the trials and tribulations that come when faced with a life-changing diagnosis. Through the book, we journey with him through his cancer battle — in the consultation room of the clinic, into the operating theatre, and at the bedside recovering in the ward.

In between, he walks down memory lane, to the time when young James was starting out in school, trying out the discus. He reminisces about the great battles of yesteryear, as he carried a nation's athletic hopes and dreams in the SEA Games field events, claiming one milestone after another. Twenty-five years after it was set, his national discus record still stands today.

This book is for anyone who may be facing a cancer diagnosis of their own, or has loved ones who are. In these pages, James shares his blueprint for facing these challenges, and I hope that you will find the strength to fight this too. We may not all be national champion athletes, but that does not mean we cannot have the mindset and determination of one.

For the local sporting fraternity, this book will bring you back to the early days of Singapore sports, and perhaps help you understand the real challenges and triumphs that marked that era in Singapore athletics. These are some of the great stories of our nation's sporting heritage.

May this book inspire a new generation of Singapore champions to achieve the unthinkable. For the patient at the start of a seemingly impossible journey, let this book help you believe.

Clinical Associate **Professor Adrian Chiow**
Head and Senior Consultant, Department of Surgery
Changi General Hospital

Preface

In January 2023, James Wong reached out to me to discuss the idea of doing a book. I knew James as a former senior and teammate with the national Athletics team. His athletic prowess and self-assured confidence were always an inspiration to the younger athletes like myself. I was intrigued by the idea and resolved to hear him out.

That's when he revealed that he had recently been diagnosed with Stage 2 Bile Duct Cancer. This revelation shocked me as I am sure it must have rattled him when he first received it. Here was the 1.90-metre giant that was arguably Singapore's greatest Track and Field athlete in front of me, pouring out his struggles with cancer as I listened, enraptured by his tale. He was a proud man who rarely demonstrated weakness. It dawned on me how much this diagnosis must have affected him for him to share his vulnerabilities with me.

He wanted to document his journey to deliver a message of hope and optimism to those who may be going down the same path as him. As I started out as an advisor to the project, the fascinating story which emerged eventually convinced me to take on a greater role in it. The project also intrigued me because it was so much more than a straight up biography of his greatest hits. There were valuable lessons on how we are shaped by our own prior experiences which can often strengthen us to meet today's or even tomorrow's challenges.

There was simply so much to tell about James' story, not just about his struggles with cancer. I often wondered what his greatest sporting achievement was. Was it his 16 medals (10 golds, four silvers and two bronzes) at the SEA Games? Or was it his joint record of the most number of SEA Games golds at the same event (nine in the discus)? Perhaps it was his stunning sports career longevity or double Hammer/Discus gold? With 26 years of high-level competition under his belt, he certainly had a lot of time to make an impression!

He had been a colossal figure and presence in the regional athletics scene. He arrived at a dark moment in the sport's history in the late 1980s. As the stalwarts of our Farrer Park golden generation began to retire in the 1970s, our SEA Games gold medals disappeared along with them. This decline reached a nadir in 1985 when Singapore Athletics did not win a single gold medal at the Games. What was initially thought to be a once-off blip quickly degenerated into a golden drought lasting almost a decade.

Amidst this dry spell, James arrived at the scene at the exact moment that Singapore athletics needed a hero and champion to turn the tide. He answered the call in 1993 by winning our first gold medal at the SEA Games in 10 years.

His inspirational victory launched a streak of nine Discus golds at the Games until 2011, unbroken save for the 2007 edition where he chose not to compete. At the peak of his powers, he was once ranked third best discus thrower in Asia (based on the season's best). As if the task of winning in one event was not challenging enough, he boasts a solitary Hammer gold in 1997 where he won a historic double at the Jakarta Games.

Through most of his career, he often single-handedly bore the weight of his nation's expectations to bring in the gold medal for athletics. His achievements firmly cemented his place in the pantheon of local sporting legends, as well as one of the most successful athletes in SEA Games athletics history.

On 7 May 2023, *The Straits Times* carried an article commemorating Singapore's 1,000th gold medal at the SEA Games.[1] It was staggering to learn that James Wong had contributed 1% of our nation's total haul at that point.

But what was just as impressive as his gold-winning feats, was the longevity of his sporting career. Making his SEA Games debut in 1987, he went on to compete at the highest regional level until his final retirement in December 2013, just one month shy of his 45th birthday. In the 26 years in between, generations of athletes had started and ended their careers while the mercurial discus thrower was bagging gold after gold in two-year intervals.

When he made his SEA Games debut as a fresh-faced teenager in 1987, he was sharing the team bus with former greats and national record holders like Haron Mundir, Ong Yeok Phee, and Tang Ngai

---

[1] Inclusive of its predecessor, the Southeast Asian Peninsula or SEAP Games.

Kin. At his final Games in 2013 in Myanmar, a certain up-and-coming youngster by the name of Shanti Pereira lined up alongside him on the Team Singapore roster.

It is just as well that his preferred event was the discus throw, a turn-based chess game of wills against his opponents, where all throwers have six attempts to assert their dominance. Rankings and medal placings often switched back and forth between throwers depending on who had the best attempt at a given point in time. At the SEA Games, James often won with his first attempt. His supreme confidence extended beyond discus competitions to his personal life, where no challenge was too daunting for him.

This assured belief in himself was tested to the limits when he was diagnosed with cancer. It was a revelation that shook the foundations of his idyllic existence, just as he thought he had it all going for him.

After recovering from the initial shock, he summoned his athlete conditioning to take the disease head on. He was boosted by the strong support of his family, capable and professional medical staff, and his own indomitable spirit that had served him well all those years.

Throughout our many conversations in the development of this project, James was mindful to emphasise that his experiences in sports had helped him weather the worst of what cancer could throw at him. It was in this spirit that we opted for a narrative approach to parallel his sporting experiences alongside his cancer battle.

He was always open about the fact that his cancer fight was his biggest challenge yet. In his own words, "When you fail in sports, you can pick yourself up and try again. But when you lose against a terminal disease, there are no second chances."

Often drawing inspiration from his triumphant battles at the SEA Games, he likened his current cancer battle to another competition where he had to come out on top — his "last gold medal" as he would like to say. This expression effectively captured the essence of his struggle and also inspired the title of the book.

As his junior in the Singapore Athletics team, James always represented a towering beacon of confidence and tenacity to his teammates. Seeing him step up to the discus ring alone at the SEA Games was almost an assurance of a gold medal. He was deadly serious when it came to training and competition. Yet he maintained a cheeky and sprightly persona off it, which endeared the public to the "Big Friendly Giant". After all, this was the man who once placed a highly publicised friendly bet with former S-League coach R. Vengadasalam (a hefty man himself) over a football match result. The loser would have to carry the winner on a piggyback ride. Unfortunately for Venga, he lost this bet.

In the development of the project, I was struck by his optimism and bullishness through it all. Despite the setbacks, he never lost hope that he would eventually come out on top, even bracing himself for a long-haul battle. I am certainly not sure I could have been this cheerful in his position.

I hope his story inspires you and it has inspired me all these years.

· Part One ·

Revelations

Chapter 1

"Why Me?"

January 2023

As fireworks and fanfare ushered in the new year in 2023, many had reasons to be optimistic in a post-Covid world. In particular, one man had much to be thankful for. James Wong Tuck Yim, arguably Singapore's most successful track and field athlete, had just about everything going for him. He had a loving family, the satisfaction of watching his children mature into young adults, and an exciting new career path awaiting him.

While waiting to start his new role at the Office of Student Life at the Singapore Management University (SMU), James even found the time to embark on trips to the Philippines and Thailand, connecting with lifelong friends like the former Thai thrower Wansawang Sawasdee who was once his fierce rival in the discus ring. As intense rivalry gave way to mutual respect and kinship forged over countless battles at the SEA Games, James now spent time with his former competitors exploring local sights and delicacies together.

Life was good, before fate dealt him a different hand.

PART ONE Revelations

Sometime after he had celebrated his 54th birthday, James started to notice that he had dark yellow urine and different-coloured stools. He also experienced persistent bloatedness in his stomach that did not go away, causing him some discomfort. He initially put it down to dehydration and went about his daily life. Since there was no pain, he did not think much of it.

But it did not go away, and his family was worried when they saw a yellow tinge in his eyes. At their urging, he visited the SMU clinic on campus after the symptoms persisted for a week. He was initially diagnosed with diarrhoea and was given some medicine to treat it. Relieved that this was all that it was, James continued with his work day as his department was busy preparing for a student event they were organising that day, and he did not want to leave the team short-handed.

Over the next few days, friends and family started to notice a yellow tinge not only in his eyes, but also his face. Convinced that something more sinister was at play, James made another trip back to the clinic. This time, he was immediately referred to the Emergency Department at the Changi General Hospital for a more in-depth examination.

There, he was subject to a series of blood tests which returned alarming results. The tests showed that James' bilirubin[2] levels were almost 10 times higher than normal levels, indicating that his body

---

[2] Bilirubin is a yellow substance created during the process of breaking down old red blood cells. It is usually concentrated in the liver and flushed out naturally if liver functions are normal.

was having difficulties flushing out the compound naturally. This hinted at the disturbing fact that his bile duct might be obstructed, affecting his bilirubin drainage and leading the doctors to diagnose his ailment as obstructive jaundice which was causing the yellowing of his skin. He was admitted to the hospital that very evening on 20 January.

The doctors now needed to conduct a thorough scan before confirming the nature of this obstruction. The issue, however, was that this took place just before the Lunar New Year weekend, and scanning facilities were prioritised for life threatening and emergency cases. In the meantime, he would be hospitalised throughout the New Year long weekend.

The wait was agonising and frustrating for him, even if he was optimistic. "Even as I was impatient to know my diagnosis, I hadn't felt any pain at all those past few weeks and didn't think it could be anything too serious," he recalled.

Although he could not partake in the New Year festivities, he kept himself occupied in his usual outgoing manner by chatting with the nurses and other patients who spent the lonely New Year with him in the hospital ward. Whatever he was going through was just a temporary inconvenience to him.

After an agonising weekend and New Year holiday of boredom, James could finally look forward to his long-awaited CT scan. What was uncovered by the scan was more troubling than the initial diagnosis. The initial CT scan identified a mass at the bottom of the

PART ONE  Revelations

bile duct close to the pancreas duct, leading to concerns about the nature of the tumour.

In order to determine this, an oral scope was arranged with the intentions to check for any obstructions, as well as to perform a biopsy of the tumour to establish whether it was benign or malignant. The scope procedure also involved an insertion of a temporary stent in his bile duct to bypass the blockage of the tumour, restoring the flow of bile and thereby relieving the symptoms of his jaundice.

The results of the biopsy were made known to James the following day. The obstruction in his bile duct was found to be cancerous, leading the doctors to quickly conclude that James had *cholangiocarcinoma*, or a cancer of the bile duct.

Although not one to give in to despair easily, this diagnosis still hit him like a freight train. Time in the doctor's office slowed to a crawl as James' mind was flooded with questions that he had no answers to. How would his family take it? Would he follow in his father's footsteps, who passed away from cancer as well? If it was terminal, how much time did he have left? How was his family going to cope without him? Why did this happen to him? And why now?

Looking at the pamphlets and visual diagrams that the doctor had laid out before him to help explain his condition, his mind went into a muddled blur and his unshakeable confidence started to momentarily waver. The towering former athlete, who once pushed the discus distance at the SEA Games to new limits, was now brought to his knees by a cancerous cell no more than 2 centimetres in width.

Jana, his wife, reflected on the whirlwind two weeks that the family had experienced. "We didn't think too much of it at first. If it was obstructive jaundice as the doctors initially thought it was, it was a condition that could be easily treated. Even during the New Year when he was warded, we thought he would bounce back after that like he always did."

To compound his misery, he developed pancreatitis after the bile duct stent insertion, which was now causing him an untold amount of pain after the procedure. He was stricken and bedridden for four whole days before it subsided.

"Initially, I didn't feel anything," he recalled. "Then it got progressively worse that evening to the point that I couldn't move. I was in agony the whole time. I could not eat, drink, or even move around. I was breaking out in cold sweats to the point I blacked out for a few hours before the resident doctor came and checked on me. This was easily one of the most painful sensations I have felt in my entire life. I felt like I got stabbed and couldn't breathe or move without experiencing an acute pain tearing through my left abdomen. It was just terrible." For someone who is no stranger to pain, the amount of discomfort James must have felt was unimaginable.

A year that looked to open new doors and opportunities for James quickly descended into anguish within a short span of two weeks. With surgery looming in a month's time, James had to dust off that familiar iron will that had served him so well in his glittering 30-year career as a national athlete to confront this setback.

Chapter 2

"This Seems Fun."

January 1969

James' rise to prominence would in many ways mirror his sudden change of fortunes in 2023. He was born in 1969, the fifth of six children (three elder sisters, one older and one younger brother) to a shipyard blacksmith and a homemaker. James spent his childhood growing up in the workers' quarters opposite Keppel Shipyard. The tiny one-room apartment housed his entire family of eight.

His family was not wealthy, but his parents worked hard to put food on the table. James could not recall a time when his family had to go hungry because there were too many mouths to feed. In a Mother's Day newspaper interview much later in his adult life, he paid tribute to his parents' frugality and careful financial planning which enabled them to provide as best as they could for all their children.

While his childhood home has since made way for more modern developments, James would still delight in pointing out where his former home used to be, situated near the foot of one of the cable car towers, whenever he passed by the area with friends. He also retained many fond memories of his Telok Blangah neighbourhood as well as the unstructured games he would play with his neighbours and siblings.

"There was huge concrete *longkang*[3] right behind my home. It was always exciting when it rained. We would use our crude engineering skills to dam up the drain with canvas tarps and we would have our very own swimming pool with fish to catch. Those were delightful moments!" James would recall with a tinge of childlike glee.

While children of today would have their free time packed end-to-end with sports, music or speech classes, and tuition, catching spiders, climbing frangipani trees, and fishing were James' preferred dose of enrichment while he was growing up in the 1970s.

James first tried his hand at organised sports when he was studying at Labrador Primary School. There, he tried out

Fishing and swimming were favourite pastimes of James in his youth.

[3] Drainage ditch.

PART ONE Revelations

different games like softball and football, never really settling on any particular sport. This carried on until he was at Pasir Panjang Secondary School,[4] where he first laid his hands on the wooden metallic disc that would change his life forever.

"It was the Annual School Sports Day and my House was looking for participants for the throws event. Someone suggested that I should give it a go. My physical education teacher Mr. Mohamed Abdullah gave some simple pointers to guide me. Without much effort, I hurled a 22-metre effort with a wooden disc and came in second. I still wasn't particularly drawn to the event at that point in time, but I found it fun nevertheless."

It was at this point that James' elder brother Eric, also in the same school, suggested that James drop by the then Kallang Practice Track (now the Home of Athletics) to seek proper instruction. Eric had on occasion been at the track to run with some of his friends and had seen a group of throwers practising there. Life was simple for students like James back then. Lacking any sort of serious hobbies after school or any real direction in life, he agreed to give it a try.

On a sunny afternoon during the June school holidays of 1984, James took a bus from his school in Pasir Panjang that brought him to the Kallang Practice Track. True enough, he saw a group of throwers practising with a Caucasian coach. Mustering his courage,

---

[4] While Pasir Panjang Secondary School no longer exists, it has certainly made its mark on Singapore's sporting history. Apart from James Wong as one of its distinguished alumni, the school can also lay claim to another local sporting legend: a certain small-statured sprinter by the name of C. Kunalan.

"This Seems Fun."

James was an active young student who partook in sports any chance he got. Standing on the left, he was already towering over his peers at a young age.

In his spare time, James (bottom right holding the gong) would seek out activities like joining a lion dance troupe as a cure for his restlessness.

PART ONE  Revelations

James strode up to the group to introduce himself. Impressed by his fearlessness as well as his strapping 1.86-metre frame, the coach agreed to let him join the group.

The coach Gary Stenlund, had represented the United States in the 1968 Mexico Olympics in the javelin throw. After his competitive days, Stenlund reinvented himself as a successful coach and was invited by the then Singapore Sports Council (SSC) to Singapore on a three-month coaching stint as part of the SSC/A&W Athletics Training Scheme to develop athletic talents. The plan was for Stenlund to coach local throw talents and impart his coaching wisdom to local coaches, who would subsequently take over at the end of his three-month stay.

James recalled his first experience with structured training: "I didn't understand the mechanics of throwing at the start. I just flung the discus as far as I could. It felt good and I was enjoying myself at the same time. Under Gary, I began to comprehend how good technique could make all the difference."

In those few months, James would improve by leaps and bounds, leaving a profound impression on Stenlund. In an interview with *The Straits Times* before he left, the American coach identified two local throw talents for future greatness. One was javelin thrower Ng Bock Huat, and the other was James, the young boy who showed up only a month or two prior. After his departure at the end of August, James and his throwing group were left in the care of local coach Fok Keng Choy.

"This Seems Fun."

The late Dr. Tan Eng Liang, Chairman of the SSC and the architect of the SSC/A&W Athletics Training Scheme which James became a part of, presenting an award to the beaming young athlete at one of the programme's events in 1984.

The scheme that started it all. It was through this programme that James' talent in the discus was identified and developed.

Chapter 3

The Killer Instinct

The hard work that James invested in his newfound hobby soon began to pay off, as he started dominating the local meets he signed up for. From November 1984, less than half a year after he started training competitively, the records began to tumble like dominos. In dashing style, the towering teenager spun and hurled the circular disc further and further at each subsequent meet, decimating age-group and meet records along the way while unleashing his trademark roar after each attempt. This roar would soon become synonymous with his emerging athletic prowess and confidence.

By April 1986, almost two years after the day he first picked up the discus at a school meet, James had written himself into local athletics history by becoming the nation's best ever discus thrower. He obliterated the national record by more than a metre when he recorded a 41.56-metre throw. Incidentally, the previous record was held by his own coach, Fok Keng Choy.

The Kallang Practice Track became almost like James' second home as he dove headlong into his newfound hobby.

A beaming Coach Fok told *The Straits Times* after the feat that he knew it was only a matter of time given how rapid his protege's improvement had been at training. From this point on, the record never left the massive palms of James Wong as he endeavoured to push them further to unimaginable limits over the next decade.

The experience of undergoing a structured training programme with a coach and training mates was an exciting one for James. "Training and competing were much simpler in the 1980s. There was no Internet or other sources of training information readily available. We depended a lot on Coach Fok for guidance. His training regimen included a mix of throws practice and gym work. We even had a session where he made us run the 300 metres 10 times!

PART ONE  Revelations

We were training up to six times a week and never ever questioned him. The coach was the authority and we complied with whatever he made us do."

In interviews conducted with *The Straits Times*, Coach Fok spoke of James' initial "shy" nature and the innovative means he had to employ to bring out his "killer instinct" that was not yet second nature to the young thrower. This may be hard to believe for those who knew the discus champion at his prime and were so used to seeing the ease with which he conversed and interacted with the media, friends, and competitors alike.

In the same interview, James acknowledged that he had to raise his game mentally. He was still young and had a long way to go. "I know that during a competition, everything is different. You may be friends outside the ring, but the reason you are there is to win. So if I push you, you go down. If you push me, you go up. Everybody's trying to shove each other off the rostrum. At the 1986 Junior World Cup in Athens, I really felt it. Nobody was there for fun, everyone was dead serious."

James also explored his personal motivations for picking up the sport in those earlier years. "I wasn't the best student in school and didn't have any serious hobbies. Neither did I have any inspirational figures to keep me motivated. Training then was just about meeting friends and passing time together. If you told me back then how my career would pan out, I would be very surprised indeed."

A little-known fact about James' involvement in school sports is

Apart from athletics, football was James' next love. His impressive height and quick reflexes accorded him natural advantages as a goalkeeper.

PART ONE  Revelations

that he also represented his school in football[5] where he played as a goalkeeper. "Football was my other love and I thought I was actually pretty good at it, perhaps due to my agility and quick reflexes. I once scored a goal from my own half as a goalkeeper! Ask my former teammates about it!" he declared with almost as much pride as when speaking of his athletics achievements.

James even attended the national team age-group try-outs in football but he ultimately did not make the cut. Football's loss was athletics' gain.

In June of 1987, he crossed a significant milestone that hinted strongly at his potential to excel beyond the national stage. At the Federal Territory Championships held in Kuala Lumpur, James heaved the discus to 47.98 metres. While it was yet another routine national record for him, he also surpassed the SEA Games record by 20 centimetres. It was then held by Zaw Weik of Burma, who incidentally set the record in 1969, the year James was born.

This made everyone sit up and take notice. The boy who was previously breaking age-group and national records for fun was suddenly the best thrower in Southeast Asia, at least on paper. Talk inevitably shifted to his potential for the gold medal at the SEA Games held in Jakarta in three months' time.

While the pressure built up on James' broad shoulders, he exuded a surprising air of serenity and calmness, especially for someone who

---

[5] In the early 2010s, James gathered a group of current and former national athletes to form a football team that played a few friendly games against other teams.

was thrust in the limelight so suddenly. "I knew there were expectations, but it's all part of the sport. If you want to excel in this, you need to deal with it, for better or worse."

This stoicism has characterised James' approach to adversity throughout his competitive days, even with a different struggle decades later.

James spinning the discus to yet another National Schools Track and Field Championships record in front of a packed National Stadium.

Chapter 4

The First of Many

The 14th SEA Games in 1987 would be James' first experience in a major games competition. Sporting long flowing locks that reflected his optimism and confidence, he felt that his preparations were complete. While already a mainstay with the national team, the experience would still be an exciting one for the 18-year-old. James was held in awe at the opening ceremony hosted in the vast construct that was the Gelora Bung Karno Stadium. He would also enter the competition with equally huge expectations placed on him to deliver Singapore's first athletics gold medal at the Games since K. Jayamani's marathon effort in the 1983 edition held on home ground.

With his usual fearlessness, he went toe to toe with the best discus throwers from the region but ultimately came up short of the gold. It was a massive disappointment for the debutant when he finished in third place with a 44.82-metre throw. Singapore athletics' gold medal drought would be extended by another two more years at least.

Reflecting on that moment years later, James recalled, "I wasn't scared or awed by the expectations and occasion. I just needed more experience throwing at major meets and big stadiums. While disappointed, I was confident it would come eventually."

James made two revelatory discoveries almost 40 years apart: his sporting talent and cancer diagnosis. He first realised his love for the discus event, which ultimately honed his competitive instincts. Confidence, fortitude, and unwavering optimism were all developed after decades of hard work in the discus ring and gym. The aimless, drifting teenager was given a sense of purpose in competitive athletics.

Even if James endured an underwhelming SEA Games (by his standards) in his debut, his achievements after three years of competitive training had already surpassed that of some seasoned national athletes' entire careers. In the discus event, he held the records in the under-15, under-17, and under-20 age-group categories. He was also the National Schools Track and Field Championships record holder in the A Division[6] category. He was the first Southeast Asian junior athlete to throw beyond 50 metres (with the 1.5-kilogram implement). He was the ASEAN Schools Track and Field Championships record holder, had surpassed the SEA Games record distance, and had broken the national record an eye-popping five times — and he was just getting started.

---

[6] For the age group between 17 and 20 years of age.

PART ONE Revelations

A beaming James standing atop the winner's podium after breaking the ASEAN Schools Track and Field Championships record in 1987.

· Part Two ·

The Hunt for Glory

Chapter 5

"Acceptance, then Adaptation."

February 2023

"Mr. and Mrs. Wong," Dr. Adrian Chiow of Changi General Hospital (CGH) addressed James and Jana in a sombre voice. "It is my recommendation that Mr. Wong will need to go for surgery upfront. This is not just to remove the tumour, but to also determine if the cancer has spread to the surrounding organs. We would like to do so at the earliest opportunity with your permission."

Dr. Chiow had called for a meeting with James' family to discuss the implications surrounding the Whipple surgery that was required. He could not offer any guarantees for success, only that surgery had to be done before the cancer had a chance to spread.

The Whipple procedure is a complex surgery. As the pancreas resides deep in the abdomen, a series of careful incisions have to be

PART TWO  The Hunt for Glory

made in order to get to the pancreas and remove the tumour. Tests will then have to be conducted on the surrounding organs to ascertain if they are cancer-free. It is not a simple surgery and requires about six to eight hours to complete.

It was a clear decision for James and his family. He was no stranger to adversity and challenges at the highest level. This would be yet another one for him.

To seek reassurance of his chances, James resolved to ask his surgeon, "Doctor, how experienced are you with this sort of thing?"

"Well," the doctor paused and looked at him, expressionless. "It's not my first time, but it will be my second."

There was an awkward tension before the doctor's stoney expression gave way, and his lips slowly curled up into a reassuring smile to his patient. The tension broken, James then understood that it was a silly question to ask. His surgeon is the Chief of Surgery and a Senior Consultant of Hepatobiliary and Pancreatic Surgery with the Department of Surgery at CGH. This was well within his subspeciality experience and James knew he was in good hands.

Before his discharge, James had to meet with the CGH rehabilitation medicine team to determine his physical readiness for surgery. He was subjected to some physical tests and was given an order to lose weight, gain muscle, and improve his overall fitness to not just prepare for surgery, but also to act as a buffer for the inevitable atrophy that would occur to his muscles as he lay in bed for his post-surgery recovery. With surgery fixed on 24 February, he had about three weeks to get into shape.

The fighter in James Wong was not about to throw in the towel just yet. "To peak for a major competition like the SEA Games, I would need a full season or two of preparation. Now I had three weeks to prepare for the fight of my life. It sounded like a challenge and I was game."

It had been some time since James had any physical exercise. His last competition outing was the Singapore Athletics Inter-Club Championships held in October 2022. He competed in the hammer throw event and finished second in a field of open competitors. He was 53 years old at the time!

James did not waste any time. Drawing from his experience in competition planning and preparation, what followed was a routine familiar to him. He sat down and slowly mapped out his exercise regimen for the next three weeks. He would start off with brisk walks to get his heart rate up and try to lose excess weight. He would dabble in some strength work, starting with bodyweight exercises with plans to move up to gym work should his physical condition allow it.

His son Jordan, then enrolled in the Diploma in Food, Nutrition & Culinary Science course at Temasek Polytechnic, chipped in to help his father with nutrition planning. According to the doctors, James required about 150 grams of protein in his daily intake. Jordan saw to the calculations to ensure that his father received his protein from the right sources like salmon, eggs, and lean meats.

Jordan recalled the experience of supporting his father's nutritional

PART TWO  The Hunt for Glory

needs: "It was difficult at first because my father is someone who enjoys eating. But once he got into the routine, there was no stopping him."

Now it was just a matter of putting the plan into action. Tapping into his former athlete discipline, James designed a spartan routine which involved daily exercise, meals, and rest. Everything was meticulously planned with almost clockwork adherence to the schedule.

"I started with brisk walking around my neighbourhood. At first, it was tiring and I was aching badly from the lack of exercise before that. But I knew my body's physical adaptation would soon take place and I would get better at it."

After digesting the bad news, James would embark on a punishing exercise regime to get into shape for his surgery.

"Acceptance, then Adaptation."

Jana Lauren-Wong, ever the supportive wife, accompanied James on many of his exercise sessions to keep him motivated.

He started to push his distances and walking speed to the point where he was able to perform a slow jog. Taking time off from work, Jana and Jordan were there on some occasions to encourage him, pace him, and walk or jog with him. Right before the surgery, James was clocking 40 minutes for a 5-kilometre run. Though far from Olympics standard, this was no less impressive for a man who, by his own admission, "didn't enjoy jogging very much".

James experienced the same gains with his strength. Starting with bodyweight exercises, he quickly progressed to the stage where he was able to bench press up to 80 kilograms and leg press up to 200 kilograms for 10 repetitions each.

PART TWO  The Hunt for Glory

When news started to spread about James' medical condition, he was quickly inundated with requests to catch up or to visit his home. It started to get overwhelming for him after a while.

"While I appreciated all the well-wishes and offers to meet up from friends and family, it soon came at the expense of my daily exercise routine which was the priority for me at that point in time. Then I had an idea. If my friends wanted to catch up, they could

James being assisted in the gym by his Singapore Management University colleague and former teammate Wong Yew Tong. He found that the best way to keep up with meet requests from friends was to invite them to join his exercise sessions.

accompany me during my daily walks. That way, I could complete my exercise and chat with old friends at the same time."

James also found it onerous to keep repeating his medical situation to the numerous well-wishers who came by. He decided to use WhatsApp, the phone message application, to send periodic updates to his inner circle.

When he first resolved to get in shape, James weighed 126 kilograms. By his final pre-surgery medical appointment, he had dropped to 121 kilograms. Detailed scans were also taken to determine his readiness for surgery and the results were positive. Scans seemed to indicate that the cancer cells had not spread. His bilirubin levels were back to normal and, largely as a result of consistent exercise, his heart was also healthy and strong. His doctors declared him ready for surgery. It was a remarkable demonstration of resolve for the former discus champion to go from a sedentary lifestyle to a training routine again.

He reflected on his personal motivations through it all:

"My approach to setbacks is simple. Bad news will always hurt. You have to be devoid of emotion to not feel vulnerable the way I did after hearing my diagnosis. You can allow yourself some time to mope, then you must accept your fate. Only after acceptance can you start to find solutions to your problem. That was what I tried to do with my exercise and dieting. That was adaptation.

"My philosophy to training is always to push to the

PART TWO  The Hunt for Glory

next milestone. If I can only lift 100 kilograms today, I will always look to test myself at 105 or 110 at any next opportunity. If I fail, I will try again the next time. And when I finally do it, what used to be my limit will suddenly become much easier. Then I look forward to the next peak to scale. We continually improve by pushing ourselves, not by staying comfortable."

James also set his own affairs in order. Contacting a lawyer, he made preparations for his will so as to ensure that his family would be well-provided for should anything untoward happen to him.

On the night of 23 February, James turned in early as he would do the night before competitions. He had done all he could to prepare himself for his big day. As he lay on his bed staring at the ceiling, his mind was swirling with thoughts on how his surgery would play out. He was also reflecting on his physical routines over the past three weeks, satisfied with how it had worked out for him. Eventually, his thoughts drifted to his preparations from a distant age, a time when he had to make drastic changes to his training and lifestyle in order to win an elusive prize.

Chapter 6

Close, But Still Not There Yet

January 1988

Fresh from his maiden SEA Games in 1987, James underwent some changes that would affect his training preparations for the upcoming SEA Games. Firstly, he parted ways with Coach Fok and began working out with his training partner Ng Bock Huat, a former national javelin thrower.

Then he enlisted for National Service, an obligation required of all healthy Singaporean male youth regardless of their social standing or ethnic-religious background. Initially a driver, James reached out to benefactors from the Singapore Amateur Athletics Association (SAAA), namely Lieutenant-Colonel Kesavan Soon (a former Olympian and then vice-president of the SAAA) and Major George Abraham (who was sitting on one of the SAAA's sub-committees). They were able to transfer him to clerical duties which would allow him to train uninterrupted.

PART TWO  The Hunt for Glory

However, James was still unable to witness any major breakthroughs in distances during the lead up to the 1989 Kuala Lumpur SEA Games. Nevertheless, he was regarded as Singapore athletics' best chance to win their first SEA Games gold medal since 1983, when SAAA president Loh Lin Kok first took the reins of the association.

In his way stood veteran Thai thrower Adul Kerdsri who had won every gold medal in the event since 1983. James would have his work cut out for him.

At Kuala Lumpur's Merdeka Stadium, James dug deep to find the inner strength required of him to fling the discus to 47.96 metres, two centimetres shy of his national record and his best throw in two years. It was, however, not enough to upstage the Thai defending champion who hurled a 48.04-metre attempt, beating him to the gold by 8 centimetres. James had to settle for silver this time.

"I suffered from a lack of experience throwing at a big stadium. The construct and architecture of each stadium is different, and it does affect the way wind is channelled to the competing arena. Throwing at a covered stadium like this and at an open field for training are two very different situations entirely. Most of the time, you need to qualify for major competitions to be able to throw in big stadiums. That was something I lacked. Despite this, I was satisfied with the result. I thought that Adul was lucky to beat me and I felt closer to the gold."

It was at this point that James decided he needed a dramatic change to his training scenery if he wished to make that much-needed breakthrough in performance. He started to cast his gaze overseas, specifically to the US which was largely considered a powerhouse in athletics.

In a September 1990 interview with *The Straits Times*, he confessed that he "needed a greater injection of expertise and more push in training". He went on, "I broke the national record three years ago but I've not been able to better that. It was heartbreaking and I feel like I have more to offer, like to throw 55 metres and be of Asian standard. That is why I've decided that going overseas is the best option for me."

James already knew some of his teammates who were training and studying in the US. They included pole vaulter Ng Kean Mun, sprinter Prema Govindan, triple jumper Francis Nathan, and high jumper Jim Hui. He was particularly intrigued with the athletics programme at Mt. San Antonio College in California which offered him the opportunity to pursue a pre-university diploma to help him bridge the gap to a possible university degree in the future. He held extensive conversations with both Francis and Jim, who were based there, about training and living in California.

Help also came from another familiar source. Singapore middle-distance legend Chee Swee Lee, who was based in the US and working as a college recruiter for prospective foreign students to study there, was available to lend some assistance to James to facilitate his big move. Incidentally, she was also a distinguished alumni from Mt. San Antonio College.

PART TWO  The Hunt for Glory

Seeking help with funding, James, who did not come from a well-to-do family, reached out to the sporting authorities as well as his own sponsors before a tripartite agreement was concluded between the Singapore Sports Council, SAAA, and his own sponsor Newk Plus Four, the local distributor for the Italian sports brand Lotto, to cover his annual $24,000 tuition fees. The support came rather easily since the nation's hopes were pinned on him to deliver the gold at the 1991 SEA Games. Everything was now set for him to make the move.

Chapter 7

New System, New Adjustments

The big leap to the unknown was exciting yet demanding for the young James Wong, who was only age 21 at that point in time in 1990. Enrolled in a course that would get him an Associate of Arts diploma when he graduated, he confessed to struggling with the change of scenery in the initial days.

"I came from a big family and there was always companionship and food for me when I got home from training. Now I had to take care of daily necessities like cooking and laundry, on top of my studying and training. I didn't know how to cook and it was tough getting used to American-style food on a daily basis. In my phone calls home, most of the conversations with my mother would centre around cooking recipes and how to prepare certain dishes that I missed."

His cooking skills would soon improve alongside his throwing

PART TWO  The Hunt for Glory

ability to the point that he was confident enough to whip up curry dishes, briyani, and even chicken rice. He later joked in an interview that apart from graduating with his degree, he also obtained an unofficial "Diploma in Asian Culinary Skills". Thus began his lifelong love affair with cooking, a hobby he still enjoys today.

Apart from cooking, James also missed other comforts from home, especially the safety and stability. He was close enough to Los Angeles to feel the impact of the Rodney King Riots in 1992 which tore through the city, prompting a friend to lend him a handgun for protection. This brought awareness of the violence home to him in a very personal way, something which he expressed discomfort with. Besides this, he also lived through hail storms, tornadoes, and earthquakes, something which he would never have experienced in sunny Singapore. It all added up to make his adjustments to living alone that much harder.

On a more personal note, James was also faced with academic challenges.

"Studying was not something that came naturally to me. I struggled academically back in secondary school and came to the US with only a GCE O-Level certificate. But I recognised that I had no choice. I was here on a scholarship paid for by generous sponsors and I needed to get my diploma. Without it, I could no longer train. If I persevered in my school work, it was only because I wanted to compete."

On the training front, on the other hand, James relished the

New System, New Adjustments

opportunity to test himself against a higher calibre of throwers. He was working with former Nigerian Olympian Grace Apiafi and the differences in training culture were telling.

"Training was much more structured in America. There were frequent team meetings which addressed everything from competition schedule, training plans, student well-being, to discipline issues. Training and competition attire and shoes were also provided, and there was even a kit manager who made sure all the athletes' training attire needs were managed. Everything felt ordered and organised, and although this was just a college team, we felt part of a professional sports set-up.

"I also had the opportunity to train and observe discus throwers who were putting out distances above 50 metres frequently. It was an eye-opener to gain insights from them as well as to train with them. The college also had a repository of VHS tapes about throwing mechanics and competitions. We could simply loan them out to view at our leisure. There was no Internet or YouTube in those days, so these resources were invaluable to help athletes like me improve back then."

Despite his initial struggles, James demonstrated a determined resolve to adjust to his new circumstances. It was for this reason that he decided to opt out of the 1990 Beijing Asian Games, which would have been held one month into his school term.

Eventually, the friendly giant's outgoing personality became the key catalyst to help him through. He also started to see unexpected

PART TWO  The Hunt for Glory

positive outcomes on the academic front as well.

"I found that, just like sports, if I put my mind to it, I could actually do pretty well at school. I especially appreciated the autonomy given to students to select their own courses and how they wished to complete them. I also enjoyed the freedom of living on my own."

James recounted a story of when he took a Speech 101 class and was asked to make a class presentation on a topic of his choice. Naturally, he chose to describe the discus throw. Halfway through his presentation, he scanned the room and realised he did not have the class' attention. He decided to switch his approach. Twisting his torso into a pre-throw position and taking in as deep a breath as he could, he spun into a mock throw and at the same time, unleashed a deafening bellow as with what he would have done for a competition, except this was in an enclosed lecture theatre. There was not a single sleepy eye in the room after that.

Having his family over also aided his adjustment. James' parents were extremely proud of their son who was the first member of the family to enrol in college and took the opportunity to visit him. Being among familiar faces again did lighten up his mood, and the thrower has fond memories of his family's visit.

"I drove my parents to Las Vegas so we could spend some family time there together. It was their first time in America. I learnt how to gamble on the trip and got so lucky at playing Craps that I won over $300, which essentially covered the cost of our Vegas trip.

"I remember during the trip that my father complained of the cold since he could not get used to the chilly weather. I then handed him my college jacket so he could keep warm. He became so fond of that jacket that he brought it back to Singapore and was frequently seen wearing it. I guess it was also his way of showing how proud he was of me. Since that jacket became a prized possession of his, we cremated it with him when he passed away years later of cancer."

On the sporting front, James was regularly pushing 50 metres in his training throws, once even going up to 53 metres, but he had yet to do it in a competition to make it official. The college had a most innovative way under Coach Don Ruh to encourage their throwers to improve their versatility across all the throws. A 'Throws Pentathlon', would be held periodically where the champion would be the thrower who could record the best performances across the shot put, hammer, discus, javelin, and 35-pound kettlebell throws. The rationale was to improve talent identification. Coach Ruh would tell his charges that they never knew what they were good at until they tried it. It was through these sessions that James discovered that apart from the discus, he was pretty handy with the hammer as well.

For the casual observer who has never seen the hammer throw in action, the event is a spectacle to behold. It requires the thrower to fling the hammer implement as far as possible after a series of rotational spins to gather momentum. The hammer in question is actually a solid metal ball weighing 7.26 kilograms (the weight for the men's event) with a handle that is attached to the ball via a metal

PART TWO  The Hunt for Glory

wire. The event requires not just strength and power but also good technique, balance, and sense of timing, not just to excel at it, but also to prevent serious injuries. There are inherent dangers to practising the event, especially if one is unskilled and untrained. This is part of the reason why there were few practitioners of this art at the local level as safety became a growing concern. But it is truly a fascinating event to witness.

Singapore has enjoyed a storied history in the event with hammer greats like Eknath Mane and Sankaran Gawade striking gold at the SEA Games across the 1960s and 1970s during the 'Golden Age' of Singapore Athletics. Now James had joined this select group of bold Singaporeans with the hope of emulating their illustrious achievements.

On the strength of his impressive training performances, the Singapore Amateur Athletics Association decided to nominate their discus champion for the IAAF World Athletics Championships held in Tokyo in August 1991. The Championships was the biggest competition for James at the time and a perfect tune up for the upcoming SEA Games to be held in Manila at the end of the year.

While he had an eye-opening experience watching the top throwers throw beyond 60 metres, he had a pedestrian outing by his standards, recording 44.26 metres in the discus and 46.04 metres in the hammer events, never progressing beyond the qualifying rounds. Putting his disappointment aside, his sights were now firmly planted on the SEA Games.

James with Yu Long Nyu (far right), national heptathlon record holder at the Tokyo World Athletics Championships in 1991.

Chapter 8

The "Flop"

Expectations were now sky high for James to get the gold medal in the 1991 Manila SEA Games. There was talk of him getting the bronze in 1987, then silver in 1989, and the gold which should naturally be next. His encouraging training performances only fuelled the intense speculation and placed the weighty burden of the gold squarely on his shoulders.

However, James was at pains to explain what happened next. He fell short of even a medal in both the discus and his newly adopted event, the hammer, finishing in fourth place for both events. For the first time, the word "flop" would be used to describe the thrower's performances, an experience which he confessed was a low point in his storied career.

James conceded that he was distracted. "I was on a scholarship and I wanted to graduate in order not to let my sponsors and family down. This balance between studies and sports was not something I managed very effectively at that point. While training was going well, I felt that it was still not at a level to help me with my breakthrough."

At the Singapore Amateur Athletics Association (SAAA) Annual Dinner and Dance event later that year, President Loh Lin Kok even singled him out for criticism, lambasting the thrower's "lack of focus and commitment" in front of a gathered assembly of athletes, coaches, officials, and journalists, much to James' public embarrassment. While he held his silence this time, President Loh's direct confrontational style would one day reach a tipping point, causing both administrator and athlete to clash publicly.

Owing to his underwhelming SEA Games performance, James was faced with a financial setback. The SAAA and Singapore Sports Council both informed him that they were withdrawing his scholarship. At this point, he only had six months left before graduation. It was a most ironic and unfortunate development, since one of the reasons for his performances suffering was the additional time he spent on his studies. However, James lucked out when his corporate sponsor Newk Plus Four decided to pick up the tab, but not without seeking assurances that the athlete would deliver a much better performance on home ground at the 1993 SEA Games.

In desperation, James even tried his hand at American football in a bid to secure a football scholarship. This was after he was told that his size, strength, and speed were attributes that were suited for the rigours of the game. After trying his hand at a number of different positions, he concluded that the game was not for him.

PART TWO: The Hunt for Glory

In search of funding for his studies, James turned to American football in hopes of winning a football scholarship.

After his graduation from Mt. San Antonio College, James sought to achieve a number of things. He wanted to move on to pursue a degree and, at the same time, seek a suitable high-performance training venue which would allow him to push his training to a new level and redeem himself at the SEA Games.

He eventually settled on Angelo State University in Texas after doing his research. It was a college that suited his training (since it had a dedicated throws programme) and academic needs. He would pursue a Bachelor of Science degree in Kinesiology there. Financially, Newk Plus Four agreed to cover half of his tuition fees, with James forking out the remaining sum from his own pocket. The sponsorship had one clear and unmistakable condition: he had to deliver the gold medal in 1993.

Training levels at Angelo State were at an intensity James had not experienced before. The college's training facilities were top notch, capable of hosting major competitions like the NCAA Division II Championships. He was rubbing shoulders with throwers who could go beyond 60 metres with the discus, some of whom were Europeans who were more than happy to share training tips and knowledge with him. As meals were provided, James found that he had more time to spend on his books and training since he no longer needed to cook. It was a refreshing change for him. By then, he was more experienced with training and living on his own overseas, and was in a better state of mind to push the envelope of his performances.

It did not take long for the floodgates to open.

PART TWO The Hunt for Glory

James in his dormitory room at Angelo State University. It was his first time staying in a campus dormitory.

Within a span of two months in early 1993, the towering thrower obliterated three national records in the discus, shot put, and hammer events in a stunning statement of intent for the upcoming SEA Games. He also broke the 50-metre barrier for the first time in the discus when he flung it 51.02 metres across a Texas field. In the hammer, James recorded 55.38 metres, which was 14 centimetres behind the SEA Games record held by Malaysian Wong Tee Kue. This set up a realistic prospect that instead of one gold, James may end up with two at the Games.

Chapter 9

A Shiny Piece of Metal

Expectations were building up for James yet again. Even more so since Singapore was hosting the 1993 edition of the SEA Games. It had been a decade since athletics last won a gold medal at the SEA Games. The drought was weighing heavily on the Singapore Amateur Athletics Association (SAAA) officials and also on James, the man with the best chance of ending this barren spell on home ground.

Learning his lesson from 1991, he diverted any discussions about his medal chances and simply told the media that his "actions would do the talking for him".

"I could see what the gold meant for the athletics fraternity. Any official, coach, or athlete I spoke to all told me the same thing: they hoped that I could get the gold. This was what it meant to carry the nation's expectations. I was not prepared to let them down."

PART TWO  The Hunt for Glory

James also needed the gold medal for personal reasons. His sponsors had been nothing less than generous with him. But this charity could not go on indefinitely. He needed a result to repay the unwavering faith they kept with him. If he lost this sponsorship, he would have to give up his college education as there was no way he could afford the tuition fees all by himself. The stakes were high and it was do-or-die for him.

To up the ante, local distributors representing Coca-Cola and Asics both offered up a cash incentive totalling $20,000 for the gold, should James be good enough to get his hands on it.

In order to optimise his preparations, the SAAA decided to fly him back for the Games at the last possible moment, a week before the start of the competition. By the SAAA's admission, they did not have the technical expertise to support his training back in Singapore. Hence, he would be better served by working with his coaches at Angelo State until he had to compete.

The Kallang National Stadium, or the 'Grand Old Lady', held a special place in the hearts of all Singaporean athletes at the time. Originally built in time for the 1973 SEA Games, it eventually played host to numerous sporting, political, and entertainment events, creating many special memories for athletes and spectators alike from the Malaysia Cup nights to the National Day Parades. It was meant to be a symbol of post-independence optimism, and it would now play host to the biggest regional sporting event, the 1993 SEA Games, as it did back in 1973 and 1983.

A Shiny Piece of Metal

This significance was not lost on James. The stadium held a special place in his heart as well. He had watched a number of football games as a schoolboy there. When he became a member of the national team set-up in athletics, he spent countless hours training and competing at the main stadium and its gym facilities. He was more than determined to add to this special significance with a performance for his nation to remember.

The hammer event was first on the schedule for him, a perfect warmup for the discus thereafter. Though close to the SEA Games record, he was not the favourite. This chasm in class was clearly laid out when reigning SEA Games champion and record holder Wong Tee Kue served up another record-breaking special by pushing his SEA Games mark to 58.50 metres, out-classing his Singaporean opponent who towered almost a full head over the Malaysian.

James in action at the SEA Games hammer event in 1993 where he clinched a silver medal. The Games also saw the debut of his iconic headband, an accessory he would wear for major competitions throughout the 1990s.

PART TWO — The Hunt for Glory

James could only manage 52.86 metres for the silver medal.

The only other medal of the day went to female marathoner Toh Soh Liang, who engaged in a thrilling neck and neck battle with her Indonesian rival, only to fall behind the leading pace at the 35-kilometre mark to settle for silver.

So it was two silvers for Singapore athletics on day one of the competition. The gold was still nowhere in sight. Nervousness started to set in at the Singapore camp.

James was unfazed, however. The hammer throw, after all, was not his focus. In an interview with *The Straits Times*, he conceded that "this was just my third year with the event. Technically, I'm still not good enough."

He was now more determined than ever to win the discus event. In an assured demonstration of his supreme confidence, while waiting for the bus to the National Stadium at the hotel lobby, James told President Loh Lin Kok that he would bring home the gold for Singapore.

There was a two-day interval between the hammer and discus events, of which the latter was scheduled at four in the afternoon, where the local crowds could pack the stadium to see their hometown favourite.

As luck would have had it, when the athletes were warming up, the heavens opened with flashes of lightning and cracks of thunder. Before long, a heavy downpour followed and the organisers had no choice but to postpone the event till eight in the morning the following day, much to the disappointment of the gathered spectators.

There were even casual whispers of supernatural powers conspiring to prevent Singapore athletics from winning its coveted gold.

But any talk of divine conspiracies was quickly silenced when James strode up to the discus ring the next morning for his opening throw. Over his forehead strapped a bandana which held his flowing locks back. Although not a religious person, he drew inspiration from the biblical tale of Samson, the strong man who derived his inhuman strength from his long hair.

Performing a few warm-up swings with his throwing arm to feel and acclimatise himself to the weight of the discus, his mind was laser-focused at the task at hand. Without warning, he launched into a rapid spin, gathering speed with each rotation. To the casual spectator, the sight of a 110-kilogram thrower executing a pirouette at such velocity seemed to defy conventional physics. It was a breathtaking display of grace, agility, and power, all wrapped up in a single package that was James Wong.

At the final spin, he brought his trailing right throwing arm to the fore and gave a final heave to spin the discus out with his fingers. What followed was a thunderous cry that reverberated around the Kallang Stadium and silenced the home crowd.

The disc shot out of his hands like a rocket, slicing through the air at a steady trajectory before landing near the 50-metre distance marker placed on the field to help throwers gauge their distance from afar. Once the measurements were taken, the scoreboard read:

PART TWO  The Hunt for Glory

49.02 metres. It was his best-ever distance at any of his SEA Games, and it was only his first throw.

His competitors were rattled. At each subsequent attempt, James unleashed his discus with a triumphant howl, as if to announce that he was ready to assume the mantle of champion. His fierce competitors Adul Kerdsri and SEA Games discus record holder Fidel Repizo of the Philippines simply had no response to the younger challenger's growing confidence. He led the standings from first to the sixth and final throw and was never in any danger of being deposed from his perch.

After his final throw and knowing that the victory was certain, James reached into his bag and pulled out a red and white flag, adorned with a crescent moon and five stars. He carefully unfurled it, before hoisting the Singapore colours over his shoulders, to the cheers of his parents, the stadium crowd, and journalists that were present. After 10 long years, Singapore athletics finally won its first gold medal. A new discus champion had been crowned, a crown that James would not relinquish for years to come.

At the medal ceremony when *Majulah Singapura* finally rang out at a SEA Games athletics event for the first time in a decade, the magnitude of his achievement finally caught up with James. Listening to the anthem on the podium and reflecting on the struggles he had endured to get to this watershed moment, he suddenly experienced a cathartic purge as his emotions overcame him. He began shedding tears of joy and relief, the first time Singaporeans would catch a

A Shiny Piece of Metal

James all smiles on the podium as he wins Singapore athletics' first gold medal at the SEA Games since 1983.

glimpse of the unflappable 1.90-metre giant in a rare show of emotional vulnerability.

There was a noticeable change in mood at the Singapore Athletics camp after this historic gold. While the media painted comparisons about the state of athletics against swimming, that was bagging gold after gold, it was a sobering reality of how far the sport needed to

PART TWO   The Hunt for Glory

The pride of the nation. James is congratulated by senior athletics officials and competitors. From left, Maurice Nicholas (vice-president of SAAA), Adul Kerdsri (silver medallist), Loh Lin Kok (president of SAAA), James, and Fidel Repizo (bronze medallist).

progress. But this did not dampen the spirits of James or the athletics fraternity.

Hamkah Afik, a sprinter at the 1993 Games, would often delight in recounting how the *Majulah Singapura* which was played at James' victory ceremony right before his own 200-metres finals event inspired him to push past his rivals and win an unlikely silver medal.

Leslie Shepherdson, a member of the SAAA Management Committee and a former jumper back in his competitive days, extended an invite to James and some of his teammates to his own pub, called the Honky Tonk, for a celebratory drink.

"Bring your medal!" he told James. "Drinks are on the house."

James did not require a second invite. That evening, he got so drunk that teammate and high jumper Wong Yew Tong had to carry him back to his hotel room, much to the annoyance of national head coach Qi Zutan who was waiting impatiently at the lobby for his charges to return after their unsanctioned excursion.

"At its most basic form, the medal is just a shiny piece of metal. But I could see the significance of it to so many people. People came up to me and wanted to see or touch it. They wanted their photo with me, or even my autograph. I think it also instilled a belief in the athletics fraternity that we can rise from the ashes again after 10 years without a gold. That was special to me, that I could be the one to bring this hope to the sport."

The hard-won gold medal for Singapore, the first of many to come for James.

23 February 2023

James lay on his bed, his mind laden with thoughts on his past and present, as his eyelids grew heavier by the minute. But instead of worry and anxiety, his final thought before succumbing to sleep was one of confidence.

· Part Three ·

Onwards, to Victory

Chapter 10

"I've Done All I Can."

24 February 2023

A piercing alarm woke James up from his sleep at six in the morning. Although this was his usual routine, the day was anything but business as usual. After washing up, he headed to his kitchen for a glass of water, the only nourishment he could ingest since he had to adhere to a mandatory fast. After getting dressed, Jana drove him and his daughter Jessica to Changi General Hospital.

Jessica had been working in Germany for some months and had flown back for her father's surgery when she heard the news. Jordan, a member of the national volleyball team, was away with the team at a competition held in the Maldives. His parents originally made plans to travel and support the team, but they were cancelled after James' diagnosis. Jordan wanted to stay by his father's side, but was persuaded by his parents to carry on with the trip since his team was also preparing for the SEA Games held in Cambodia later that May.

PART THREE Onwards, to Victory

Jordan reflected on his father's road to the surgery. "I really wanted to be there for my dad. The family was so worried. But in the weeks leading up to the surgery, he was just so confident about his preparations and the outcome that it lifted the spirits at home. Throughout it all, he never wavered, not to the family at least. That was the inspirational effect he could have on people around him. We were all still worried, but deep down we knew he was going to pull through."

The family reached the hospital at about 7.30 in the morning where James was immediately admitted. After filling out the necessary paperwork, he was made to change into his patient gown and brought to a waiting room with his family. There, they exchanged hugs and James reassured his family.

Jessica had bought a little stuffed angel figure from Germany for her father. There was a message on the packaging that read in German, "*Ich pass auf dich auf*" or "I'll watch over you". Although her father was not the sentimental sort and had laughed the gift off when he first received it at home, she knew it meant something to him when she saw that he had brought it with him to the hospital.

James then had a short call with Jordan before handing over his mobile phone to Jessica with instructions to update a carefully selected contact list of family and close friends about the surgery and recovery process. Then his family had to leave him to be processed for surgery.

Left to his own thoughts, James' imagination started to run wild,

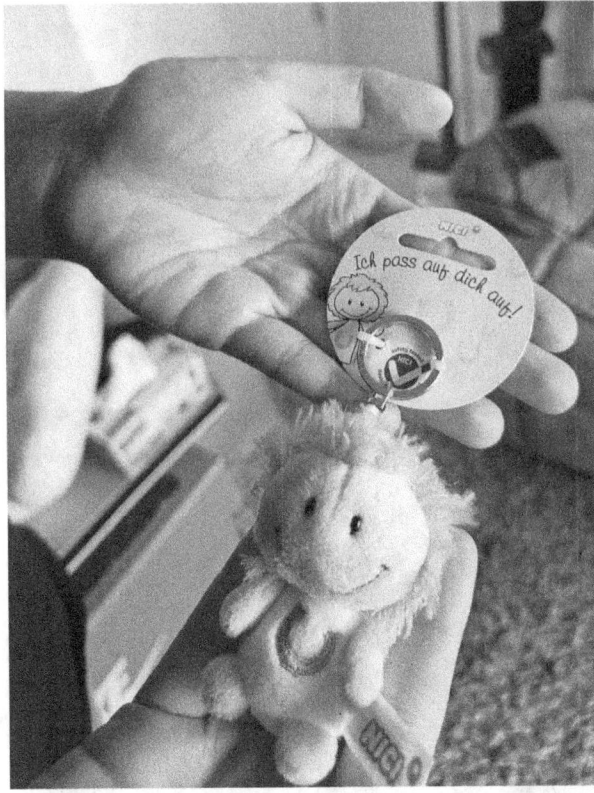

"I'll watch over you", Jessica's good luck charm for her father gifted on the day of his surgery.

chipping away at his usual stoic veneer until it revealed a rare moment of weakness and anxiety. He asked to see his surgeon Dr. Chiow once more. As the doctor entered the room, James reached out to grasp his surgeon's hands.

"Doctor, please do your best. I entrust my life to you."

The surgeon clasped the patient's hands and gave him all the assurance he needed, before leaving him alone once more in the room to prepare for surgery.

Faced with yet another formidable challenge, James had to dig

PART THREE   Onwards, to Victory

James exuding an air of confidence just before his surgery as he is accompanied by Jana and Jessica. The family had rallied together to support him and attend to his needs during the difficult weeks leading up to the surgery. Jordan was missing from the picture as he had travelled with the national volleyball team to the Maldives with his parents' blessing.

deep in order to invoke his own mental preparations which had always calmed him in the discus ring across countless SEA Games. He reflected on his own training and surgery preparation over the past month and felt a sense of reassurance that he had done all he could. It was now down to Dr. Chiow and his team to pick up where James had left off and carry him to the finish line.

In the meantime, his family left the hospital and spent the day in restless anticipation of the surgery outcome.

Jessica recalled her experiences that day. "My mum and I just tried to pretend that everything was normal. We went for our meal and talked about everything else except the surgery. Try as we did to distract ourselves, the thought of my father was always lingering in the recesses of our thoughts. I know my mum felt the same way. But neither of us brought it up."

Finally, the time came for him to be wheeled into the operating theatre. He looked up at the room clock, it was about nine in the morning. After performing routine checks on his identity and the nature of the operation, the hospital orderlies wheeled him out of the waiting room. On his bed, James stared listlessly at the endless panels on the ceiling, which resembled a conveyor belt delivering him to his destination.

As his trolley bed entered the operating theatre and he was wheeled into position, the nurse switched on the surgery lamps and his eyes squinted from their brilliance. For the briefest moment, he was reminded of the harsh glare of the Bukit Jalil Stadium spotlights in

PART THREE  Onwards, to Victory

Kuala Lumpur which were trained on him as he stepped up to the ring.

He was soon greeted by the anesthesiologist who once again rattled off the routine pre-surgery questions which James had grown accustomed to answering without a second thought. The anesthesiologist then explained to him how exactly he would administer the anaesthesia to him, namely, by gas through a breathing mask.

The nurses then proceeded to fit the mask over his face. He felt suction in his ears. His skin broke into goosebumps from the cold. His heart pounded like drum beats. Then there was calmness, silence, and darkness.

Chapter 11

The First Graduate in the Family

June 1993

It was just a shiny trinket, but the hard-won discus gold medal opened up doors of opportunities once again for James.

Symbolising the aspirations of the athletics fraternity, the medal was supposed to kickstart Singapore athletics' long-awaited return to the Farrer Park heydays of the 1960s and 1970s, where Singapore athletes dominated the SEAP (Southeast Asian Peninsular Games) and later SEA Games. It prompted the Singapore Amateur Athletics Association (SAAA) to finalise the hires of foreign coaches like Kerry Hill of New Zealand and Rainer Paul of Germany to provide the much-needed injection of expertise to push local athletics back to its glory days.

For James, it helped to reinstate his overseas funding and support, where the Singapore Sports Council and SAAA stepped in to pay for

PART THREE Onwards, to Victory

his overseas training and studies at Angelo State University once more. Apart from this, he was also trying to source for more sponsors to support his training.

For now, his only thought was to quickly return to the US. For him, the hard work on his 1995 title defence needed to start immediately. After soaking up the adulation from his victory for two weeks, James was back in Texas.

His first thought was to prepare for the upcoming Asian Games in 1994 that was to be held at Hiroshima. However, due to a NCAA technicality, James was eventually forced to sit out the Games due to his "red shirt" status. This meant that in order to preserve his eligibility to compete for his college, he needed to abstain from competition for a year. Seeing that he needed to complete his degree and was training under the college's programme, he had little choice but to prioritise the college's needs and forgo the Asian Games. This would make it the second Asian Games in a row that James would be missing.

On the training front, however, he continued to improve steadily. He was averaging throws of mid-50 metres in training and was getting stronger and more powerful.

By the summer of 1995, he had broken his national records a stunning nine times across the three throw events of shot put, hammer, and discus. In what was his final competition representing Angelo State, James took part in the NCAA Division II Track and Field Championships and finished fourth in the discus and third in

Representing ASU, James finished fourth in the discus at the NCAA Division II Track and Field Championships in 1995, earning the Division II "All-American" status.

the hammer. There he broke his hammer national record once more with a 56.36-metre hurl. In a buoyant mood, he declared to the press that he would be attempting a triple gold medal hunt at the SEA Games, competing in the shot put, discus, and hammer.

As James' American journey came to its conclusion, he was reflective of his four years in America.

> "I come from a simple family and had very little aspirations in life. The sport of athletics opened doors for me I would never have had if I hadn't made that journey down to the Kallang Practice Track in June 1984 to try my luck.

PART THREE Onwards, to Victory

A proud moment for the Wong clan as James becomes the first university graduate in his family.

The First Graduate in the Family

Because of athletics, I was able to travel and study overseas, to obtain a degree that made my family so proud.

"I was not a good student in secondary school. I struggled with my subjects and was not outstanding in any particular way. Even as I managed to cope with school work at Mt. San Antonio, it was because they covered mostly fundamental preparatory courses in general maths, science, and languages. At Angelo State, it was different. Since it was a degree programme, we went in depth into subjects like anatomy and physiology, all of which I struggled with. I even failed the compulsory American history course on my first try as I only had a vague understanding of American culture.

"Eventually, I had to devise new study methods to help me get through school. I treated schoolwork the same way I approached training in sports: with hard work and determination. People only saw the degree I got in the end. What they didn't see was the grind I put in just to pass my courses. When I finally graduated, it vindicated my belief that hard work will always pay off in some way, as long as you are willing to put in the required miles and not give up.

"As a teenager, I could not have imagined that I would become the first university graduate in my family. But it made them all so proud. This, to me, was an achievement that rivalled my sporting accolades."

Chapter 12

Willkommen, Herr James Wong

As James' graduation neared in May 1995, talk invariably centred around the future training plans of Singapore's top track and field athlete. When he was back in town, James sat down with Kerry Hill, Rainer Paul, and Ong Yeok Phee, the general manager of Singapore Amateur Athletics Association (SAAA) and a former national sprinter, to discuss his future.

They discussed options ranging from staying on in the US, training locally, or finding a new training camp entirely. Finally, it was Paul's recommendation that won the day. Hailing from the former German Democratic Republic, or more commonly known as East Germany, Paul was acquainted with Gerhard Böttcher, a discus specialist coach who was working with some of Germany's top throwers. They agreed that his training camp in Germany would be an ideal place for James. James concurred with this assessment since German throwers were world-renowned for their throwing ability. The SAAA supported this stint as a longer-term strategy to help their star athlete raise his competitiveness in time for the 1998 Bangkok Asian Games and 2000 Sydney Olympics.

With the plans finalised, James was so excited to begin this new phase that he arranged to fly off to Germany just within a week after his graduation and return to Singapore in June 1995. This was a significant milestone not just for him, but also for Singapore athletics, since he would be the first full-time professional athlete supported by the SPEX 2000 initiative. Launched in 1993 in conjunction with the SEA Games that Singapore hosted, it was a financial aid package to support the aspirations of local athletes to help Singapore achieve its sporting goals. Behind the allure and glamour of this title were clear and unmistakable performance targets that the thrower had to meet. He not only had to retain his discus crown at the SEA Games, but also had to challenge the best in Asia by the end of its three-year duration.

The training base was situated in a city in former East Germany called Halle. When James landed at the airport in Berlin, he was received by his soon-to-be coach Gerhard Böttcher. The duo proceeded to make the two-hour drive to the training camp.

Immediately, the challenges of training in Germany became apparent to James. Being an outgoing extrovert, he had always found it easy to make conversation and friends with those around him. With Coach Böttcher, there was a problem: language. The German coach only had a very limited understanding of English and James spoke no German at all. James recalled the resulting car

PART THREE   Onwards, to Victory

ride to be a very awkward experience.

The Singaporean quickly overcame this language barrier by hanging out with the younger throwers who had a better grasp of the English language. He learnt some German from them as well until he was capable of some basic communication with Coach Böttcher and the other coaches.

Before he left Singapore, James was also warned by officials that he should manage his expectations about the training and living conditions, given the location of the facility in the former Communist half of Germany. This piece of advice only helped to soften part of the blow of what he saw when he got there.

"When I got to the training centre, I was definitely taken aback to see how decrepit the buildings were. The hostel where the athletes lived could be best described as spartan. The room was big, and it had a wooden bed with some basic furniture like cabinets or wardrobes. It was also equipped with a small refrigerator and television set. Everything was old, including the room heater, wall switches, and plugs. The rooms looked like they were trapped in a 1970s time stasis, since most of the furniture or fittings seemed to date from that era. I was made to constantly relocate my room due to repair works that had to be carried out on damages. At one stage, I stayed in a dorm with no personal toilet or shower facilities in my room. If I needed to go to the loo in the middle of the night, I had to walk to a nearby public toilet. Imagine trying to do so in the dead of winter!"

James also had to get used to living and training in harsh conditions like in heavy snow. He recalled not being able to feel his fingers and the discus on occasions during winter training.

Adapting to European cuisine also presented another challenge. As he explained in a letter written to *The Straits Times* shortly upon his arrival in Germany, "The Europeans like to eat cheese, ham, and salami which I found to be rather tasteless. Coming from Singapore where our cooking is rich in spices and flavour, this required some adapting to. When I'm bored of the food, I would treat myself to a nearby Chinese restaurant or have a steak."

James experienced some challenges adapting to life in Germany. Visits like this from his sister (Hilde Wong, left) and mother (Mdm. Hoe Chew Yong, right) helped him adjust. Pictured in the middle is Coach Gerhard Böttcher.

PART THREE  Onwards, to Victory

Despite the austere living conditions, the situation with the training facilities and coaching quality was quite different entirely.

"For the first time in my life, I saw a training ground that was engineered specifically for throwers. There were no runners in sight. The throwing field was massive, about 1.5 times the size of a football field. It had four discus rings along with dedicated shot put and javelin throwing areas. The facilities were also weather-proof. There were sheltered throwing areas to allow us to throw during rainy or snowy weather, as well as gas heaters to prevent the formation of ice in the rings during winter.

"The facility was also well-stocked with equipment. The equipment room was never locked, and you could pick out anything from throwing implements to kettlebells and medicine or other training balls for practice any time of the day.

"Training was also of the highest quality. I had specialised coaches to work on my discus and hammer throws. While Gerhard (Böttcher) was a specialist with the discus, I worked with Dr. Lothar Hinz who helped me with my hammer technique. I particularly enjoyed the fact that coaches were available at the training fields all day. All we needed to do was to make a training appointment by writing our names on a piece of paper, and we would have 'booked' a training slot with our respective coaches.

James was deeply impressed with German ingenuity in throws training. Here he is pictured with a discus orbit machine, designed to help throwers mimic the spinning arc in the discus throw.

Using this method, the coaches were able to work with up to 20 throwers in a single day.

"I've always known about the German ingenuity and attention to detail in athletics, but I was not expecting this. All these far exceeded my expectations and I've never seen anything like it in all my travels for training or competition."

James also recalled being impressed by the meticulousness of German high-performance planning.

PART THREE Onwards, to Victory

"At the institute, the training programmes were planned in four-year cycles, designed to help athletes peak at the Olympics. Each year, there was a different focus, be it strength, power, or technique, and there were specific milestones or performance targets to meet before you could move on to the next stage. Each training stage was built on the fundamentals taught in the previous stage. It was all very neatly planned out and you felt like you were in good hands."

James was also exposed to a far higher level of training quality than he was used to. The Germans were highly technical in their approach to throws and he was made to unlearn and relearn much of what he once believed to be conventional knowledge in his approach to throw technique.

It was hardly surprising then that his performances enjoyed a further breakthrough when he set yet another national record, his 10th of the season across all throws, this time in discus where he swung the disc to 52.98 metres at a meet in Norden, Germany. This was a mere two months since he started his German stint. He was more than ready for the SEA Games in December 1995.

James with Coach Böttcher during a training session.

Chapter 13

The Defending Champion

Entering the SEA Games chasing after his first gold medal and doing so as defending champion were two entirely different propositions for James.

"When I was in the hunt for that first gold medal, I was hungry and desperate to get there after failing to do so on three previous occasions. As defending champion, I had to fend off the challenges from throwers who were hungry just like me back in 1993. But I wasn't really thinking about them. My goal was to throw as far as possible, and let them worry about me. It was between me and the throwing implements.

"Of course there was pressure. I was now a professional full-time athlete with the Singapore Sports Council under the SPEX 2000 programme which was supporting my training and livelihood.

PART THREE Onwards, to Victory

Besides, the Singapore Amateur Athletics Association was also paying for my hammer coach Dr. Hinz to be at the Games. I had to deliver."

Outwardly, James steered clear from making any predictions about his medal chances. To the media, he gave a cagey response.

"Anything can happen in sports. The only time I will be sure [about winning] is when I have completed my six throws, and when my opponents have completed theirs."

Fortunately for James, the discus was first on the schedule. It was an event he was confident in, and putting in a good result could possibly set a positive tone for the rest of the Games.

The Southeast Asian discus scene was in the midst of transition at the Games, which was held in Chiang Mai. Former veterans like Fidel Repizo and Adul Kerdsri who had set the standards in the 1980s and early 1990s were either retired or enjoying their swansong. There were also new challengers to the scene like the up-and-coming Thai youngster, Wansawang Sawasdee, who would go on to forge an intense rivalry and friendship with James much later. The only constant was the Singaporean James Wong, who not only seized the title at this critical transition point in an opportunistic fashion, but also served as a sort of bridge between the generations of throwers. Still only 26 years of age and with his peak years ahead of him at this point, James was already a seasoned veteran at the SEA Games, having made his debut in 1987 and competing in every Games since then.

Stepping up to the discus ring at the spanking new 700th Anniversary Stadium built just in time for the SEA Games, James

The Defending Champion

got off to a sluggish start with a 47.88-metre effort, falling behind Indonesian Ismail Sroyer. This clearly demonstrated that victory at the discus was not a done deal for the defending champion, despite his recent good form.

However, James quickly recovered, growing from strength to strength, eventually hurling the discus to 49.88 metres on his fifth throw for his second discus victory and leaving Sroyer with the silver medal. It was not the 50-metre blockbuster that he was used to throwing in Germany, but it was good enough for the win. Unknown to many until it was revealed by Kerry Hill to the press, James was

James raises his arms in victory as he is featured on the cover of SAAA's official magazine *Adrenaline* after successfully defending his discus crown at the Chiang Mai SEA Games in 1995.

PART THREE  Onwards, to Victory

actually suffering from diarrhoea for several days, which undoubtedly affected his performances.

James felt a familiar swell of pride standing on the podium as *Majulah Singapura* rang out for the first time at the stadium as he received his medal from a familiar face, Mr. Abdullah Tarmugi, Singapore's then Acting Minister for Community Development.

Proudly, he declared to the press after his victory ceremony, "Let's get the ball rolling!" This was in obvious reference to his other two events, the shot put and hammer.

The shot put was always a long shot for James. Although he was the national record holder at 15.03 metres, he was still some way from seriously challenging for a gold medal. The difference in standards was on full display as he fell out of the medal placings, throwing at only 14.09 metres, a full 2 metres away from the winning distance.

James quickly shifted his focus to the hammer. While he seemed like a sure bet for the discus, questions lingered over whether his improved hammer form would be good enough to upset the defending champion Wong Tee Kue. In the lead-up to the Games, both Wongs started their psychological games by avoiding and ignoring each other at the Games Village in Chiang Mai. There was a healthy respect for each other's abilities, but the pressure to win left little room for small talk and polite conversation.

When quizzed about the tension by the media, both throwers did not mince their words.

"If I want to say hi to him, I will go to him. I respect him, but I'm not in awe of him," declared James.

"Let him come to me if he wants to talk. Since he has not made the effort, I can't be bothered either," came Tee Kue's reply.

The anticipated showdown provided all the thrills and spills that justified the pre-event hype. The Malaysian set the tone by surging to an early lead with his first two throws of 54 metres with James trailing at 53. But the Singaporean delivered his riposte with solid efforts, surpassing 56 metres in his third and fourth throws, surging into a seemingly unassailable lead. Then it came down to the final throw for both men where James seemed like a sure bet for the gold. Tee Kue would have the chance to throw first before James.

As the Malaysian stepped up to the ring, he demonstrated his defending champion credentials by pulling a last-gasp rabbit out of the hat, swinging the metal ball to a massive 57.04 metres. This thrust him into the lead once more, seemingly snatching victory from the jaws of defeat.

If James was shaken at this point, he did not betray any emotion. He stepped into the ring and gripped the handle of the hammer implement with both hands until his knuckles were white. He knew he needed a Herculean reply to his rival, and his effort did not disappoint. Unleashing his hammer, he delivered it across the field to drop it at 56.68 metres — a new national record, his 11th of the season. But alas, it was not enough for victory. He was outclassed by his rival once again.

PART THREE Onwards, to Victory

Dr. Lothar Hinz, James' hammer coach watches his charge compete from the stadium stands at the 1995 Chiang Mai SEA Games.

While he fell short of his exacting standards, James still delivered his country's only gold in athletics at the SEA Games. There were reasons to be optimistic.

In an interview with *The Straits Times*, Dr. Hinz commented that James was "strong but he's got a lot to learn technically. He's got the power to throw 60 metres in both the discus and hammer over the next two to three years." With more time in Germany, the Singapore camp was confident he could continue to improve and qualify for the biggest meet on the athletics calendar in 1996: the Atlanta Olympics.

Chapter 14

The Aspiring Olympian

By March 1996, there was talk of athletics nominating a three-man squad for Atlanta. This shortlist included marathoner Yvonne Danson, along with high jumper Wong Yew Tong, and of course James.

Yew Tong had distinguished himself at the Chiang Mai Games not only by breaking the national record, but also the SEA Games record where he leapt to 2.22 metres. However, like James in the hammer, he lost in a fascinating jump duel against Malaysian Loo Kum Zee who pipped him to the gold with 2.24 metres. Danson is a multiple national record holder after some solid performances at Chiang Mai, chalking up a bronze and silver medal in the process.

To chase this Olympic dream, James' preparations back in Germany went into high gear.

"When I first arrived in Halle, the coaches were all impressed with my strength in the gym, but surprised that I couldn't throw beyond

PART THREE Onwards, to Victory

60 metres in the discus. This clearly demonstrated a problem with my throw technique. However, as the SEA Games in 1995 was approaching, they elected to focus on fine-tuning my technique without making drastic changes. Now that I have to restart my season again to look forward to the Olympics, they went right back to the basics with me. It was really frustrating for me to go back to the fundamentals again as I felt that I was already a thrower of some repute, but this was why I came all the way to Germany."

For the next few months, James found himself practising with sticks and leather balls once again in order to bridge his gaps in technique. But with the Olympics on the horizon, he knew he needed to make drastic changes in order to seek the improvements that he wanted. Any distance of 60 metres or less for the discus would not get him very far at the world's premier sporting event. Slowly but surely, he felt his technique improve and was optimistic about what he could achieve.

Furthermore, he was training in the best environment to improve. He had dedicated coaches, top-notch facilities, and even world-class training partners. One of them was the great Ilke Wyludda, a World Junior Champion, European Champion, and eventually Olympic Champion in the women's discus event. Her best recorded distance in the discus was a jaw-dropping 74.56 metres with a female implement (1 kilogram). James recalled being in awe of such illustrious company. Being in the presence of excellence day in and day out pushed him to go harder every day.

The Aspiring Olympian

Things seemed to be looking up for him, before life threw him a curveball.

In early July, a week before he was due to fly out, the Atlanta Olympic Games Council delivered bad news to the Singapore National Olympic Council (SNOC). They declared that in the absence of any athlete that met the Olympic qualifying marks, each country would only be allowed to send one male and female athlete. Danson was the obvious choice for the female athlete, but the SNOC and the Singapore Amateur Athletics Association had to make a tough decision between James and Yew Tong.

Ultimately, the selectors decided on Yew Tong based on the fact that he was closer to the qualifying mark than James. The high jumper was a mere centimetre away compared to James, who had to throw 62 metres.

James received the news while he was at Halle and it was devastating for him.

"I had already received my accreditation and team attire. My bags were almost packed and I had attended all the media events. Then I got the news. Yew Tong is a friend and I wished him all the best, but it did not make the decision any easier for me to swallow. I put on a brave front, but privately I asked, 'Why me?'"

Now there was only one other goal alluring enough for the towering thrower to channel all his Olympic disappointment towards: capturing that double discus–hammer gold at the following year's Jakarta SEA Games.

PART THREE  Onwards, to Victory

It was not long before James faced another setback in April 1997. He was at a training camp organised by his group in Namibia when he received the news. On one of his routine phone calls back to Singapore, James heard from his siblings that his father had been diagnosed with terminal lung cancer. The doctors only gave him six months to live. James was floored by the news.

He remembered being so affected and wondered if he should drop everything to return to Singapore. Being so far away, he felt helpless about the situation. His siblings ultimately convinced him to stay on and that they could help provide care to their father. But as soon as he could, he flew back to Singapore during one of his training breaks to be with his father and family.

He had tried his best to spend time with his father by accompanying him to the hospital for his routine checkups and treatments. He also accompanied his father on walks and other light exercises so he could keep his strength up.

He recalled, "It was just heartbreaking to see him in such a frail state where he was coughing blood and always in a state of weakness."

All things considered, it was a testament to James' iron will that he was able to maintain his focus on training despite what life had thrown at him.

Chapter 15

The "Lord of the Ring"

Since his hammer disappointment in Chiang Mai, James had been working hard with Dr. Hinz to correct his technique. He also shared his difficulties in trying to perfect both throw events.

"Many observers simply assume the hammer and discus are similar events just because there is a rotational aspect to them. But this couldn't be further from the truth. They are very different technically and require very specific training to master. Just because one is good at the discus doesn't automatically make them good at the hammer. It's like trying to perform at both the high jump and the pole vault. Both are vertical jumps, yet very different technically. When I announced that I was going to try for the double since 1991, not many people truly understood how difficult it actually was."

The clear sign of progress took place in a Berlin meet in June 1997 where James equalled his own hammer national record, fuelling his confidence that that was the year where he would finally take the hammer gold.

PART THREE  Onwards, to Victory

However, if he was expecting a simple cakewalk in the discus, he would be mistaken. News filtered out of Thailand about an emerging challenger. Wansawang Sawasdee was largely a bystander at the 1995 Chiang Mai Games where he won a bronze medal and was mostly powerless to stop the irrepressible march of the Singaporean powerhouse towards his second consecutive title. However, the young challenger had since gone from strength to strength. At a recent Thai competition, he smashed his country's shot put national record and breached the 50-metre mark in the discus. The Thais were optimistic that they had found their own champion to break James' burgeoning stranglehold over the event.

James took these challenges seriously enough for him to opt out of the Athens World Championships in order to focus on the SEA Games. Having consulted his coaches, they decided that he would need more preparation time for his two events and the World Championships would be an unnecessary distraction, considering he was unlikely to progress beyond the qualifying rounds.

At the Nike Singapore Open Track and Field Championships in September, James drew first blood against his younger Thai rival when he smashed his discus national record yet again with 54.08 metres against the Thai's 51.14 metres result.

There was more good news the following day when he hurled the hammer to a record 54.28 metres, almost a metre better than Wong Tee Kue's distance recorded at the Malaysia Open two weeks prior.

Buoyed by these impressive performances, James aimed a

not-too-subtle dig at the Thais for even daring to hype a new challenger in the discus. He declared to the media that "once the Games start, I will strip off my title and everyone will have a chance to take it from me. I hope the new Thai boy will not choke from the pressure that his officials are piling on him."

This time, James' quest for the double gold seemed almost inevitable. A position that was acknowledged even by the Indonesian and Thai officials, who seemed almost in awe of the friendly giant's physical prowess.

First on the SEA Games competition schedule in October for James was the hammer. If observers were expecting the Malaysian veteran to roll over for his Singaporean challenger, they would be sorely disappointed. The 1997 hammer event served up another "*Clash of the Titans*" blockbuster which saw two heavyweights at the top of their game vying for the crown.

The Malaysian veteran raced to an early lead with two 54-metre throws, but committed a foul on his third attempt. James saw his opportunity to seize the initiative and lead by slinging the hammer to 55.66 metres. Tee Kue closed the gap with a pair of 55-metre efforts on his fourth and fifth attempts, setting the stage for a nail-biting finale.

On his fifth attempt, James calmly strode into the ring. Gripping the handle of the hammer, he launched into his rotational swings,

PART THREE Onwards, to Victory

gathering speed with each turn as the momentum of the hammer took over. All the while, he skilfully maintained his balance throughout the rotations by rocking on his heels and toes in quick succession. As he reached the edge of the throwing circle, he unleashed the hammer with a majestic roar that resounded like a thunderclap across the Madya Stadium in Jakarta. He watched in stoney silence until the hammer pounded the green turf, throwing up clumps of grass and soil in all directions. The officials quickly scurried across to make their measurements while he held his breath until the scoreboard finally displayed the result: 58.00 metres. Once again, James let out another roar of approval as applause rang out all around. It was an impressive distance — not just a new national record, but also just half a metre short of Tee Kue's SEA Games record set in 1993.

Now the pressure shifted to Tee Kue, who had one final attempt to repeat his Chiang Mai miracle and salvage the crown that was fast slipping out of his fingers. The thought of the veteran snatching another victory with his sixth and final throw just like in 1995 did cross James' mind for a fleeting moment as he watched Tee Kue's hammer sail across the field. But there would be no fairy tale ending for the Malaysian this time. Although the defending champion recorded his best attempt, he could only manage 56.16 metres, effectively conceding the competition to the Singaporean. For James, his first gold medal was tucked in his bag in the most dramatic fashion.

The "Lord of the Ring"

Finally a gold medal in the hammer event after four attempts. James is on the podium here during the medal ceremony. Curiously, Wong Tee Kue, his Malaysian arch-rival in the event over four SEA Games, is standing on the winner's pedestal with him.

"I lost to the better man today," conceded the gracious Malaysian thrower in an interview conducted after their fascinating duel.

Securing the gold brought the hammer title back to Singapore for the first time since 1977. However, there was no time for James to bask in the euphoria of the moment. The discus was up next in three days' time.

His confidence was exemplified by his remarks to the press in the competition lead-up.

PART THREE  Onwards, to Victory

"I want to make the discus event my own. It'll be between me and the discus. I'm not thinking about the other competitors at all."

In comparison with the back-and-forth rally that defined the hammer event, the discus turned out to be a largely one-sided affair. The expected challenge from Thai youngster Wansawang Sawasdee failed to materialise as James utterly dominated the proceedings, winning by a healthy 2.5-metre margin. The final result stood at 52.18 metres, breaking his old rival Fidel Repizo's SEA Games record which was set in 1991 by 8 centimetres.

James was elated to have finally captured the unprecedented hammer–discus throw double on his third try.

"My training had stepped into a different gear since I got to Germany, and now I'm reaping the fruits of that hard work. Many people do not understand the inherent difficulties in training for two very technically different events. Even as a full-time professional athlete, I could only devote two days at most a week to practising the hammer. But the Germans are so technically proficient that I could feel myself getting sharper and more efficient with my execution. My confidence flowed from these improvements. Even as I was recovering from the exertions of the hammer, I could still muster enough strength to break the discus record. I personally rank this up there among my best achievements."

Breaking the record was special for James. It not only gave him recognition as the best ever discus thrower in Southeast Asia, but he hoped that his record-breaking performance would also help other

Singaporean athletes make similar inroads at the SEA Games, an endeavour that seemed to have met with halting progress since the 1970s.

It was oddly surprising that since surpassing the SEA Games record as a fresh-faced 18-year-old at a Malaysian meet in 1987, James took a full decade before he officially staked his claim to it. If there was any doubt about his ability to defend his titles, he had answered it at the Jakarta Games in the most emphatic fashion. He was now the undisputed Southeast Asian 'Lord of the Ring'.

After the SEA Games in October, James' immediate thoughts turned to his father's health. He was hit with another setback when his mother fell ill as well. While she was doing the laundry in the toilet one day, she suddenly felt weak and started to slur in her speech. She was immediately rushed to the hospital where she was diagnosed with a stroke. The months of providing care for her husband had taken its toll on the health of the elderly Mrs. Wong.

Sometime after the New Year in 1998, James' father was hospitalised for the final time. His condition had been deteriorating and the family was prepared for the worst. On 9 January, they received a call from the doctors summoning them to the hospital. All of them knew what it meant.

Mr. Wong Toon Khoon, the patriarch of the Wong family, passed away peacefully that day, surrounded by his six children and wife

PART THREE — Onwards, to Victory

A family holiday in Phuket. James was always grateful that Jana was able to meet his parents before his father's passing. From left, James mother Mdm. Hoe, Jana, James, and his father Mr. Wong Toon Khoon.

who was recovering from her stroke and was wheelchair-bound. He was 65 and had led a hard but fruitful working-class life providing the best he could for his family.

"I remember my father as a carefree and fun-loving person who enjoyed social activities and travelling after his retirement. I cherished the moments we had together, especially when he flew all the way to the US just to visit me in college. He was an avid sportsman in his youth and had always supported me to pursue my sporting dreams. What was really special to me was that he lived long enough to meet

Jana, and see me win my two gold medals at the Jakarta Games. These were important highlights in my life and I'm really glad he got to witness it."

Those two months were emotionally confusing for James. He was elevated to unimaginable heights after his success at the SEA Games, then was brought crashing down by his mother's illness and father's death. To cap off this bittersweet period of his life, the next day, 10 January, was his 29th birthday.

---

24 February 2023

"Mr Wong," James heard a muffled voice that sounded like that of the anaesthesiologist. "Welcome back. I'm happy to share with you that the surgery was a success!"

The patient tried to lift his heavy eyelids to make sense of where he was. It was no use. Everything was a fuzzy blur.

"What time is it?" He muttered in a barely audible voice.

"Oh, it's 11 in the evening," came the reply from the silhouette beside him.

He closed his eyes again and settled back into another deep sleep.

· Part Four ·

The Tribe

Chapter 16

A Humbling Weakness

25 February 2023

When James awoke once again in the early hours of the morning after his surgery, he was overcome by a mixed sensation of pain, weakness, and numbness. Mustering his strength, he tilted his head downwards and was greeted by a grisly sight.

Instead of the sturdy body frame that had won him countless gold medals at the SEA Games, his body was ravaged by an assortment of tubes protruding from all over. A long scar ran along his midsection, from his sternum to his belly. At regular intervals, the scar was peppered with surgical staples which prevented his incision wound from opening up. He was immobilised.

At that point, he felt like a lab rat, a human test subject kept alive by a series of tubes and machines. He later found out that the different tubes served to aid his recovery in a number of ways, such as feeding

PART FOUR  The Tribe

him, administering painkillers, draining excess blood, and even allowing him to urinate.

His doctors had initially informed him that they were opting for a keyhole surgery, and would only cut him up if the earlier procedure could not get the desired results. His long scar indicated that the surgeons had gone for the latter option.

He drifted in and out of sleep the whole night, still somewhat affected by the anaesthetic drugs that were administered during the surgery.

Dr. Chiow appeared first thing in the morning to check on his patient. He congratulated James, informing him that the surgery was a success and that he should focus on his recovery.

The first three days were the hardest for him. Unable to move and in pain, he was tube fed all the while. Urinating was done through a tube and he had an adult diaper on to help with passing motion. This had to be changed regularly, which was an ordeal for James since it required him to roll over, a simple action that felt like summiting Everest at this point.

The nurses proceeded to brief him on how he could self-administer painkillers through a button linked to one of the many tubes attached to his body. Pressing the button would inject a dosage of morphine to soothe his pain. For the first couple of days, James used the button frequently as the pain was often unbearable. While this helped ease his agony, the drug induced hallucinations which caused him to see people who were not really there. This created a sense of unease for him.

Eventually, he weaned himself off the painkillers after the third day, choosing to tough it out. His athlete instincts and conditioning had taken over at this point when he decided he needed to adapt his body to the pain.

His family was allowed to visit him from the second day onwards, but it did little to improve his mood. He was grumpy and grouchy from his helplessness. He was disappointed with himself for treating them this way, as they had always been there for him. But his constant pain and drowsiness ensured that he was not pleasant company to be around. He was like a wounded bear with a nail stuck in its paw.

Jessica revealed her family's disquiet from seeing their father in his helpless post-surgery state. "When we first entered the high-dependency ward, we saw him hooked up to all sorts of medical tubes and monitors. It was heartbreaking for us to see him like this. My father always prided himself as someone who is self-reliant. I'm sure it must have been agonising for him to feel helpless in this situation, dependent on painkillers and physical assistance for even his most basic needs. He wasn't in the best of moods either. But even in his weakened state, he still tried his best to act as if it was business as usual. When he first saw us, the only thing he wanted to know was how my brother did for his volleyball competition."

On the fourth day after surgery, the situation had improved dramatically for James. He was well enough to consume clear soup. The physiotherapist also came back and encouraged him to get off the bed to move around, something he was eager to try.

PART FOUR — The Tribe

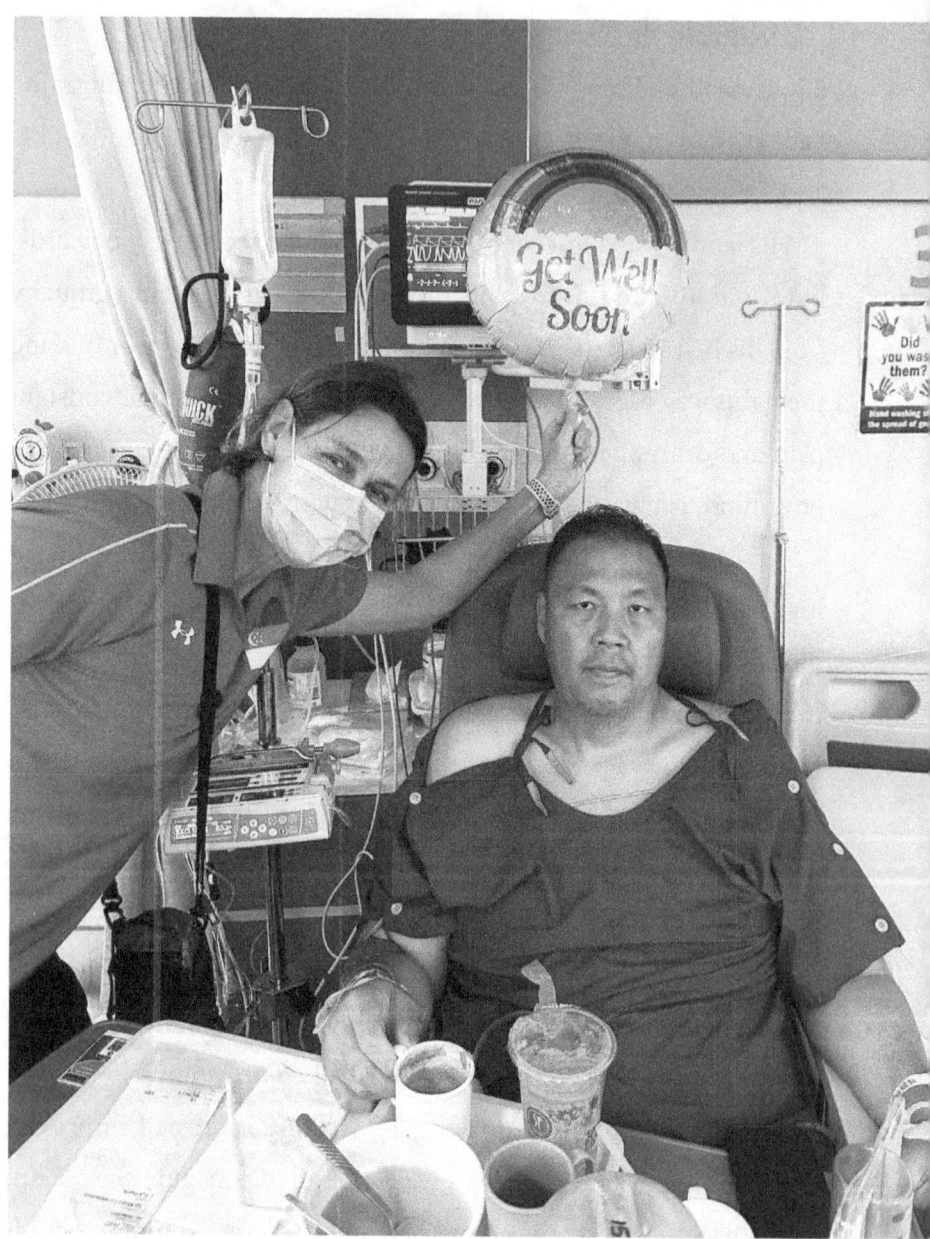

James pictured looking grumpy after his surgery. Jana was ever present by his side during those difficult moments in the hospital.

A Humbling Weakness

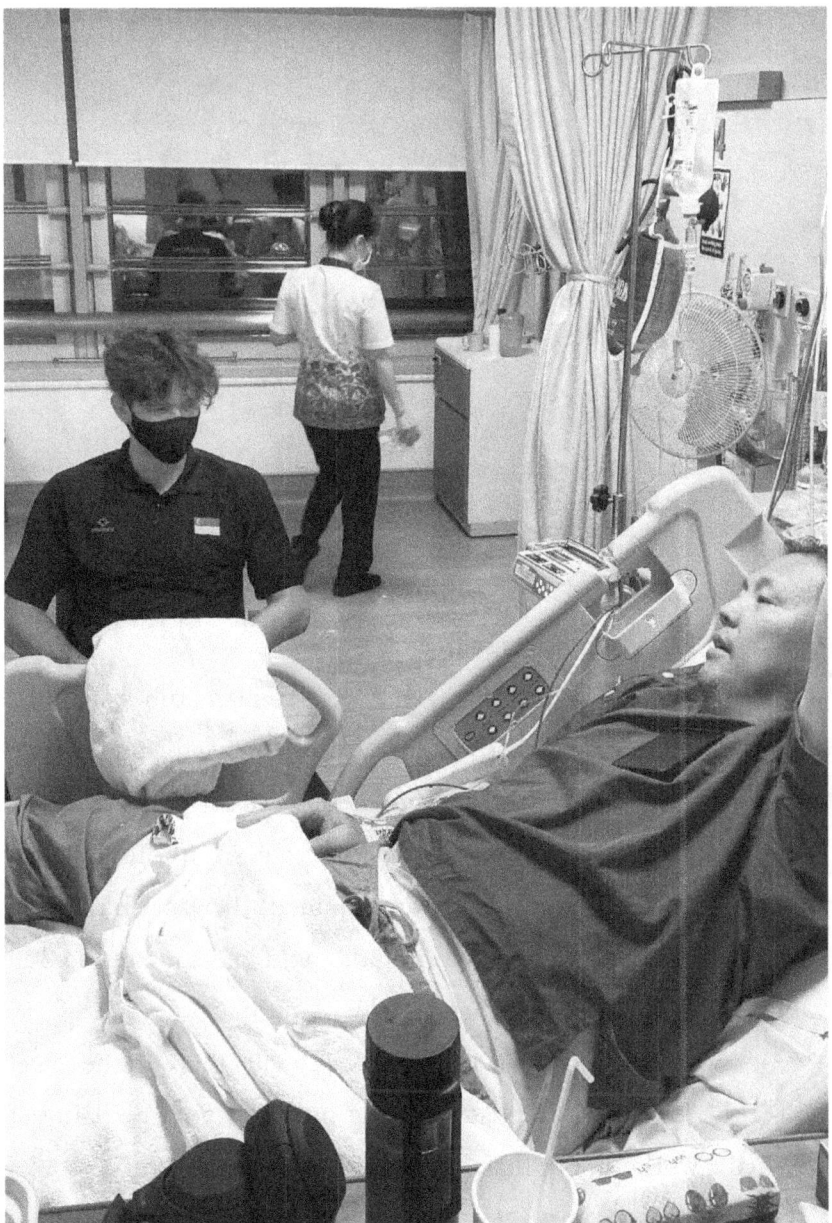

Jordan rushed to his father's side directly from the airport after his return from his volleyball competition in the Maldives.

PART FOUR   The Tribe

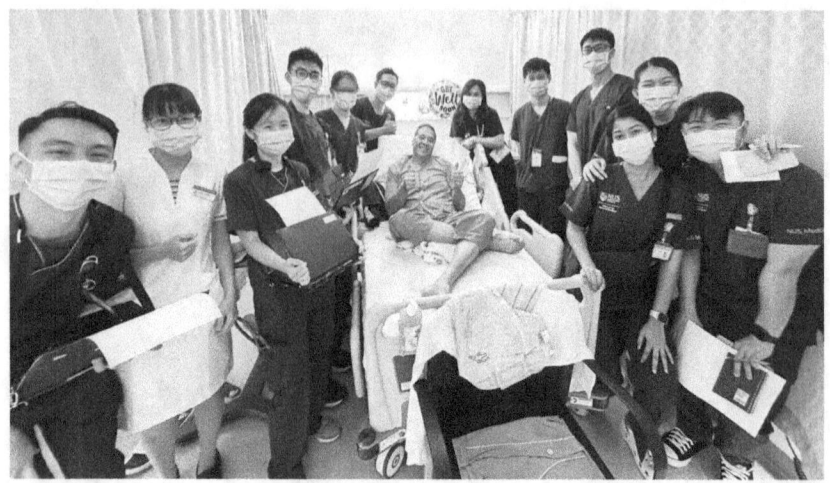

James had often spoken of his gratitude to the medical staff of CGH for providing him with the best medical care during his days in the hospital.

Shaking off the rust from three days of inactivity, James started his strength recovery process in earnest.

"It was tough just to sit up. There were so many tubes attached to my body. I needed a nurse just to help me manage the tubes while another helped me up. Just standing beside the bed was tiring. My legs were devoid of strength and they were wobbling. I felt imbalanced, like I could fall at any moment. It was a humbling moment for me. At my physical peak, I could half-squat up to 300 kilograms. Now I couldn't even stand without help."

After a few moments of standing, James finally threw in the towel and laid back down. He was sweating profusely as if he had just finished a workout. But that was not the end of his ordeal.

Sometime after dinner that evening, he started to feel a tightness in his chest. His heart started to pound so rapidly that he could feel the strong vibrations from his chest. He looked up at the heart rate monitor and was surprised to see his reading at 215 beats per minute! He was sweating and even felt like throwing up.

He immediately pressed the call button for medical attention. Before long, he was surrounded by a small army of nurses and doctors all peering at his heart rate monitor, seemingly perplexed at what they were seeing. Some of the nurses were seemingly ready for impending disaster and arrived equipped with surgical gloves, oxygen masks, and defibrillators should a resuscitation be necessary.

"Ironically, I seemed to be the only calm person in the room at first," James mused. "They were all muttering and engaging in inaudible conversation and I was just left on the bed wondering what was going on. One of the nurses told me to keep calm and not to stare at the monitors. But what else could I do? Looking at the nurses armed with medical equipment, I started to fear the worst. I informed one of the doctors to call my family even though it was late. Just in case I didn't make it out of this. I started to imagine what a person might go through in his final moments before he passes. Would I be welcomed by Ox-Head and Horse-Face, or perhaps Jesus Christ? Would I be greeted by my late father? Or would my life flash before my eyes? My imagination was running wild while the medical professionals debated over my bed."

Eventually, James was prescribed some pills for his heart. They were ultimately effective in helping to bring his heart rate down to 160 beats per minute before he was able to sleep.

PART FOUR  The Tribe

The next morning, he was once again surrounded by a band of medical professionals. This time, his surgeon Dr. Chiow was present. The surgeon then explained to him that he had experienced atrial fibrillation the night before, where electrical impulses in his heart chambers started to fire chaotically, resulting in his abnormally fast and irregular heart rhythm. He was prescribed more medicine which helped to further reduce his heart rate before it stabilised by lunch. It was a scare that barely lasted a day, but it was real enough for James to start pondering over his afterlife.

On the seventh day, James was well enough to be transferred from the high-dependency ward to a regular ward. By this point, he was able to eat solid food and perform bodily functions to a certain degree. He was also able to move short distances around his ward, mostly to the toilet. He was always accompanied by at least two orderlies, one to manage his medical tubes and another to provide physical support.

Finally on 5 March, nine days after his surgery, he was discharged after the medical professionals communicated instructions on post-surgery care to him and his family.

Once home, his family did their best to provide for him a level of care similar to what was provided at the hospital. Jessica had returned from Germany just in time for the surgery and was intending to stay for a few weeks as he recovered at home. She was able to care for her father, cooking and cleaning for him while her brother and mother were at school and coaching, respectively.

Jana and Jordan did their best to cater for James' specific post-surgery

A Humbling Weakness

James and Jana are pictured with Dr. Adrian Chiow, his surgeon. As a show of gratitude, he acquired a pair of discuses and inscribed the names of all the medical staff who had supported him before presenting it to the hospital.

dietary needs to ensure he received the necessary nutrients for recovery. When available, they accompanied him on his short walks around the neighbourhood. He even got his family to satisfy his cravings for Thai food. He was yearning for some savoury taste in his food after days of eating the bland hospital fare. While his stomach had shrunk after surgery, he still had the appetite for familiar favourites like green curry and tom yum soup, indicating that his recovery was going well.

A close-up of the discus presented to Changi General Hospital.

PART FOUR  The Tribe

"James is a foodie," Jana recalled. "Those initial days where he could not eat solid food hurt him just as bad as the physical pain from the surgery. We could see it in his mood. When he could taste his favourite dishes again, he started to perk up."

Jessica also weighed in on her family's ordeal over those few weeks. "My parents coped with what was happening through the best way they knew how. My dad is someone who doesn't like to show vulnerability. I could understand that this was part of his athlete conditioning. He kept a lot of his uncertainty, fears, and worries to himself during this whole period. He tried to pretend everything was normal, but mostly because he didn't want us to worry. I could also see how difficult it was for my mother who was very communicative and needed to express her feelings and emotions as a coping mechanism. Jordan and I tried our best to talk to her to give her this outlet now and then. I guess it helped to some extent, but none of us really had an easy time."

James was ultimately reflective of what he put his family through in those two months.

"I feel grateful to my family for putting up with me through those difficult weeks leading up to surgery as well as the days after. I must not have been easy to be around and yet they were patient with me even if they were probably worried sick. I would not have been able to go through this without their strength and support. My family has always been, and will always be, the most important thing to me."

However, recovery would prove to be an arduous journey for

James. Weeks of lying in the hospital bed and a liquid diet resulted in muscular atrophy. He had to relearn basic movements like standing up, squatting, walking, and climbing stairs. He was experiencing numbness in his legs and his weight fell to a mere 111 kilograms, the level of his pre-competitive teenage days. His surgery may have been a success, but the road to recovery would prove to be yet another challenge for him to overcome.

What gave him strength was the unwavering support of his family who helped him through this dark period, and gave him every reason to fight on. He did not always find the right words to express how he felt about them. But deep inside, he knew he could not have made it through those few months without them.

Chapter 17

The "Short Asian Man"

1995

Coach Gerhard Böttcher, in his other capacity as the German head coach for the discus, had often gathered the best throwers around the country for training camps where they could not only spar and push each other at training, but also socialise and unwind from the pressures of training and competition. In the lead up to the 1995 World Championships, he put together one of these camps in Kienbaum, a German district 40 kilometres east of Berlin.

At a dinner function that Böttcher hosted after this camp, two particular individuals stood out. One was a hulk of a man standing at 1.90 metres, the sole Asian at the party who found that his limited command of the German language was preventing him from making conversation with the rest. The other was a lanky German lady who stood at a corner and kept mostly to herself. Both of them ironically attracted attention because they were not particularly engaged in the merrymaking taking place around them.

Intrigued by the odd and unlikely couple, some athletes playfully teased the two, even going as far as to initiate a mock marriage for them.

The couple, who suddenly found themselves awkwardly at the centre of attention at the party, decided to return the favour to the rest the next morning. They borrowed a baby stroller and a doll to place inside it. At breakfast, they showed up together with the stroller in tow, drawing a mix of laughter and bewilderment from everyone in the dining hall.

This was the moment James got to know that the lady he met the previous evening was a fellow discus thrower. He also found out her name: Jana Lauren.

Born in the Communist half of Berlin during the height of the Cold War, Jana was drafted into a Berlin sports school in her early teens due to her promise shown across multiple events in athletics. The East Germans invested heavily in sports as a means to demonstrate the merits of the Communist system to the world. Jana's talent as an athlete and discus thrower was developed in this competitive system and she continued to be part of the unified German athletics set-up even after the fall of the Berlin Wall in 1989.

She had a distinguished continental career, winning the silver medal at the 1989 European Junior Championships and sixth at the 1994 European Championships, boasting a personal best of 66.30 metres.

Some time after that first meeting, Jana was pleasantly surprised when she received a call from James asking if he could visit her in

PART FOUR   The Tribe

James frequently visited Jana in Berlin and she was more than happy to play host and bring him around the city as well as its surrounding areas.

Berlin. She did not hesitate to agree and resolved to be a good host to her new Singaporean friend.

It was not long before both throwers realised that they had much in common and James' visits to Berlin became more frequent. He had just arrived in Germany at that point and was struggling to adapt in Halle. It was a small quiet town that afforded little amenities and entertainment to him beyond his training hours. Through Jana, James had an excuse to visit Berlin over the weekends where she would take him around to see the historic and entertainment sites around the capital city. Before long, they hit it off so well that they became an item.

While the couple connected easily, they had to overcome some cultural barriers. While Jana had learnt some English in school, her lack of practice made it challenging for her to maintain a proper conversation with James, who had a limited understanding of German as well. An English–German dictionary became essential for dates during those early days.

PART FOUR  The Tribe

Jana also recalled a conversation with her mother when she found out about James for the first time.

"My mother did not know where Singapore was. When she found out it was in Asia, she was horrified and asked me why I wanted to go out with a shorter man. In her mind, Asians were all small in stature. I told her to wait until she saw him in person. She wasn't disappointed after that!"

In the end, what really won her mother over was James' cooking ability. To impress Jana's family, he whipped up the classic Singaporean chicken rice to demonstrate that he was not just a star ambassador for his country in sport, but also in culinary skills. This really sealed the deal and helped him gain acceptance with her family.

Jana was formally introduced to the Singaporean public in August 1996 at the Nike Singapore Open Track and Field Championships. There was an air of excitement and curiosity among the Serangoon Stadium crowd as everyone eagerly sought to catch a glimpse of the German partner of Singapore athletics' Golden Boy. She certainly did not disappoint when she blitzed the field to break the championship and the local all-comers records to win gold on her first throw in the discus event at 57.82 metres.

Like James, she was nearly an Olympian where she missed the chance to qualify for the Atlanta Olympics by finishing fourth in the German National Championships. The top three athletes were guaranteed qualification.

She proceeded to charm the Singaporean media in a post-competition interview by rattling off a list of her favourite local dishes like *nasi lemak*, chicken rice, and *char kway teow*, which strongly hinted at the fact that her English was improving and that Singaporean fare had found a new convert.

It seemed, however, that James would not be the only one courting her, as there were whispers that the Singapore Amateur Athletics Association was seeking to persuade her, to switch citizenship so that she could represent Singapore at major competitions. Her discus prowess had stood her in good stead to win an Asian Games gold medal.

It was a decision she decided against ultimately since she was still very much interested in representing Germany in competitions.

Chapter 18

Asia and the Commonwealth Beckon

Fresh off his double gold triumph at the Jakarta Games in October 1997, James used his increased standing to raise issues concerning the remuneration of full-time athletes in Singapore. Under the SPEX 2000 programme, James was entitled to a monthly salary of $2,500 on top of his training and living expenses, which were also covered. He was also getting some financial help from his corporate sponsors like sportswear company Nike which supported him from 1996 onwards.

Additional financial bonuses came in the form of the Singapore National Olympic Council's (SNOC's) Major Games Award Programme, or MAP. Launched by former SNOC President Dr. Yeo Ning Hong in conjunction with SPEX 2000, MAP sought to provide financial incentives for Singaporean athletes to win at major games. Winning a SEA Games gold medal would grant an athlete $10,000 for example, and the quantum was scaled up accordingly to reward medal placings at bigger events like the Asian Games or Olympics.

While this looked like a tidy sum for a successful SEA Games gold-medal-winning athlete like James in the 1990s, he was quick to point out the reality behind the gloss.

In an interview with *The Straits Times* right after the Jakarta Games, he shared his sentiments on the issue: "Right now I'm not getting any CPF, no medical benefits for my family, no promotions and no bonuses. Somebody has got to help and look at this. I am after all a graduate [...] It is a big risk that I am taking, continuing with this lifestyle [...] I'm not asking for special treatment. I'm asking for equal treatment."[7]

James was already 28 years of age at this point and lamenting his lack of financial security as a full-time athlete in Singapore. It was a sentiment echoed by some of the biggest sports personalities of the day, including football legend Fandi Ahmad.

The thrower also took issue with the way the Singapore Amateur Athletics Association (SAAA) disbursed their funds to him. The money was deposited to James' bank account at irregular intervals.

---

[7] In August 2024, Minister for Culture, Community and Youth Mr. Edwin Tong took the opportunity to announce the government's enhanced support for national athletes which included CPF top-ups for high performance athletes on the Sports Excellence Scholarship to encourage sporting longevity. This belated move would have gone a long way to support James financially in the 1990s had it been introduced then, possibly even altering his sporting career trajectory.

PART FOUR  The Tribe

What complicated matters was the fact that his coaches' fees were also included in these irregular deposits. There were occasions where he could not pay his coaches simply because the SAAA did not credit the money on time, causing some embarrassment for him. Jana had to sometimes step in to help him financially on occasions.

James, moreover, took issue with the copious amount of paperwork he had to file just to process some of his living expenses claims.

"As an athlete living overseas, my focus was strictly on training. The last thing I wanted to do was to collect all my receipts even for small purchases and fill up forms just to justify why I needed the money. It was all very distracting for my training, having to worry about money and red tape all the time. I understood that I was sent on taxpayers' money, but some trust in athletes would have been much appreciated."

These financial disagreements led to showdown talks before James and the SAAA worked out an agreement. With this, he returned to Germany in January 1998 with a greater peace of mind to push towards the immediate targets laid out before him: the Asian and Commonwealth Games happening later that year.

When James first embarked on his German adventure back in 1995, one of the key long-term targets identified from the stint was for him to win glory for Singapore at the 1998 Asian and

Asia and the Commonwealth Beckon

Commonwealth Games. Incidentally, both were to be hosted in the Southeast Asian cities of Bangkok and Kuala Lumpur, respectively. For the sports administrators who greenlit his move, it was done with the understanding that he had already conquered Southeast Asia. The next logical step would be to push towards bigger targets.

James, moreover, also informed SAAA officials that, having achieved his double gold feat, he would like to drop the hammer to focus on his discus. Since both events were technically different, dedicating time for the hammer meant less time for the discus, which was his first love. He felt that with the extra time to perfect his technique, he could break the 60-metre mark. His suggestion was met with lukewarm responses from the SAAA officials who were hoping he could retain his double gold and help Singapore athletics to a respectable medal tally at the 1999 SEA Games in Brunei.

Just a month before the Commonwealth Games in August, tragedy struck. At another training camp in Berlin, James strained his right wrist tendons while doing power throws at training. He continued to train on, but only worsened the injury. After consulting the doctors, he was given an injection and told to rest. A few days later, he sought to test his throwing wrist at a competition before he heard a "pop" sound while training. This was followed by intense pain which rendered his wrist immobilised.

Arriving back in Singapore in September just before the contingent left for the Kuala Lumpur Commonwealth Games, he sought a second opinion from the doctors at the SSC's Sports Medicine Department.

PART FOUR  The Tribe

He was advised to miss the Games due to his injury.

James was disappointed, but the thought of regaining his strength and fitness in time for the Asian Games in December helped to keep his hopes and spirits up. Unfortunately, this too proved a bridge too far as the SNOC decided to drop him from their Asian Games roster upon learning that he would not recover in time.

This would mark the third consecutive occasion where James would miss the Asiad. It also strained relations between the SAAA and him, since the *raison d'être* for his overseas training stint was precisely to compete and perform at these Games. It led to questions about the wisdom of continued support for him. Tension was brewing.

For the SAAA, James' omission also presented the association with an unwanted statistic: it would be the first time in the Asian Games' 47-year history that Singapore athletics would not be fielding a single athlete. It spoke volumes of the state that the sport was in and it also hardened the SAAA's management approach towards athletes that it perceived to be under-performing.

Chapter 19

That Special "Feeling"

As if to answer his critics, James made a remarkable recovery from his wrist injury to deliver sterling results in Germany in April 1999. The extensive work he had put in to focus on his fundamentals finally started to pay off in the most dazzling fashion. At a meet in Halle where he was based, James flung the hammer to a new national record of 58.20 metres, improving upon his gold medal result in Jakarta by a fraction.

His massively improved form in speed and power was on full display at an impromptu sprint test he conducted on himself. With the help of light gate speed sensors, James powered through the 100 metres in 11.99 seconds. For a thrower weighing 120 kilograms, this was a hugely impressive time.

Since he moved to Germany, his coaches had been talking up James' potential to surpass 60 metres in the discus. While this figure may seem far-fetched to many, since he had yet to throw beyond 55 metres in competition after years of trying, James finally put his

PART FOUR  The Tribe

doubters to rest at a meet in the German town of Wiesbaden where he was scheduled to compete in the discus.

"Something remarkable happened during my warmup before the meet. While I was doing standing throws, they felt easy and effortless. More importantly, I saw the discus fly towards the 50-metre marker. Right then, I knew this was going to be my day."

Stepping up to the ring for the first throw, he proved his prediction right as he swung the discus to a new national record of 57.68 metres, improving on the previous record by a massive 3.5 metres. But he was just getting started. The records continued to tumble throw after throw, with James bagging 58 metres in the next three of four attempts.

Even then, he was not done yet. On his sixth and final attempt, James stepped up to the ring oozing with confidence from his stellar performance thus far. He took a moment to feel the wind, an important element that affected throwing performance. There was a light headwind. The conditions were perfect. He knew his moment had come.

Launching into his spin, he unleashed a mighty release as he watched the discus spin out of his fingertips. Without even waiting for the discus to land, he clenched both fists and held them in front of him with a resounding cry of victory. The release felt so good he did not need to see it land. The eventual result revealed something he had already known when the discus left his hands: it was another national record and his best ever throw yet — 59.87 metres!

That Special "Feeling"

James hurling the discus to a new national and Southeast Asian regional record of 59.87 metres at Wiesbaden.

"There are moments in sport when the execution of your technique is just so perfect that you know the result is going to be exceptional. It's like the feeling when a basketballer gets his shot technique right for a three-pointer. Or when a footballer strikes his free kick at the precise angle and force to generate the curl of the ball. You don't need to see if the ball enters the net to know it is going to be a good attempt.

PART FOUR  The Tribe

My final throw at Wiesbaden was one of those moments. I knew it was going to be special before the discus landed. More importantly, I knew from the moment the exact execution I needed to recapture this feeling, and I was confident I could replicate it in subsequent competitions."

James returned to Singapore in July 1999, just weeks before the Brunei SEA Games with a single-minded determination to chase his 60-metre target. To free himself from the weight of expectations, he embarked on a self-imposed media blackout where he refused to entertain any questions regarding the SEA Games. It was a decision that not only befuddled but also frustrated the media who were hoping to get usable soundbites from the clear discus favourite ahead of the Games.

The blackout reflected the immense pressure James must have been feeling at this point. Singapore athletics only selected a mere four athletes for the Games. Apart from James, there were distance runner G. Elangovan and high jumpers Wong Yew Tong and David Woon, all of whom were not expected to seriously challenge for gold medals. The discus giant was quite literally standing head and shoulders above his teammates at this point, carrying the hopes of athletics almost single-handedly.

The discus was scheduled for the first day of the competition and James was ready. Such was his confidence and focus at this point that he had not even bothered to see who his competitors in the start list were. As far as he was concerned, it was him against his 60-metre target.

In his opening throw, James signalled his intent by breaking the Games' record with a 54.36-metre effort. After the attempt was ratified, the stadium announcer had barely acknowledged his record over the stadium public address system before he let loose another stunner with 56.14 metres. This drew gasps from 2,000 odd spectators in attendance who were starting to turn their attention to the field rather than events on the track.

His third attempt pushed the envelope further with 59.17 metres, prompting more cheers and applause as the result appeared on the scoreboard. This time, all attention was focused on the discus cage, aware that something significant was taking place there. Film crews and journalists in the stadium were jostling for choice vantage points to capture what they knew was a historic moment.

James eased up with a pair of 57-metre throws before his final attempt. He was like an orchestra conductor at this point, directing the proceedings within the stadium, holding the audience's emotions in the palm of his hand, generating applause and cheers with his discus prowess and showmanship. He was now priming his audience for the finale of his grand opus.

You could hear a pin drop in the stadium as he strode up to the discus ring. The question on everyone's lips was whether he could breach 60 metres. With a few warmup swings of his throwing arm, he broke into his spin, gathering dizzying momentum with every rotation,

PART FOUR The Tribe

Left: James was in imperious form at the Brunei SEA Games and utterly dominated the competition. It was just him and the discus and he bagged not just a gold medal, but also the SEA Games record of 59.50 metres that is still standing at the time of this book's writing in 2024.

Right: The numbers say it all. It was rare at that time to have discus throwers throw beyond 50 metres at the SEA Games. To have someone push so close to 60 metres was almost surreal and unbelievable.

demonstrating all the grace of a ballerina with the explosiveness of a powerlifter. As his spin drew to its conclusion, he swung his mighty throwing arm and sent the discus hurtling through the air, while he released all his pent-up emotions in a deafening war cry.

James watched his discus slice through the air in a steady trajectory until it landed near the 60-metre distance marker. Cheers erupted from the stands as the crowd celebrated what was surely another SEA Games record. At this point, there was not a single soul in the stadium

That Special "Feeling"

who was not rooting for the Singaporean man-mountain. The scoreboard read 59.50 metres — yet another record, but not the 60-metre headline he was looking for.

The pressure had now been noticeably lifted off his shoulders. He was all smiles again as he engaged the media in free-flowing conversations, a stark contrast to his icy aloofness when he first arrived.

"The SEA Games record of 1999 was a special achievement for

PART FOUR The Tribe

James mobbed by a host of journalists after his record-breaking feat. He was at the height of his prowess and popularity at this stage.

me. It capped 15 years of hard work and sacrifices since I first picked up the discus. Even though it wasn't a personal best, many people do not understand that throwing in a sheltered stadium is often more difficult than in an open field. Stadiums are usually not as windy and it's harder for the discus to travel. To come so close to my personal best inside a stadium was not an easy feat to maintain."

The date was 8 August. James had delivered a birthday present to his nation on the eve of her National Day by winning Singapore's first gold medal at the Brunei Games, his fifth in total across all the Games.

Going into the hammer event, James started in the unfamiliar position as favourite. He was not only the defending champion, but also based on season standings, his national record set in April was a full two metres ahead of Wong Tee Kue's season best. It looked on paper to be a one-sided affair.

But if James' experience with the hammer had taught him anything, it was the fact that the Malaysian veteran always had the potential to conjure magical moments at the SEA Games, especially when he had his back against the wall.

James opened with a 54.66-metre effort, leaving Tee Kue trailing until his third throw, where the Malaysian police officer managed to equal James' attempt with the exact same distance. Earlier, the Singaporean had seemingly taken a bold step to securing the gold with what looked like a 55–56-metre attempt on his second throw. But it was ultimately ruled out due to a foul he committed when he stepped out of the throwing circle.

Try as he might, James could not raise his game beyond his first and best attempt as Tee Kue went from strength to strength, capping his competition with a 55.50-metre throw on his final attempt. The Sarawak native had recaptured his hammer gold from James.

Tee Kue's unexpected victory left the Malaysian camp jubilant while the Singaporean officials and journalists were reeling in stunned silence. *The Straits Times* published a full-page image spread which summed up the gloom. It depicted James dragging his hammer on the ground as he was leaving the throwing cage, looking disconsolate. He stared into space for some time before he got up to fulfil his media obligations to the horde of journalists waiting to hear from him.

PART FOUR   The Tribe

James in action with the hammer. Exhausted by his exertions in the discus, he was outmatched by yet another virtuoso performance from Wong Tee Kue.

While he was happy to talk to the press two days prior, the same experience felt like a burden now.

"It was never a sure thing," he told them. "Which was why I didn't want to talk to the press before the Games. It was just not my day. I would like to apologise to those who put their faith in me."

While James knew he had not paid as much attention to the hammer, losing it was still disappointing considering his pre-competition form in relation to his opponent's. Even his Malaysian rival had words of sympathy for him when he told *The Straits Times* that "perhaps the discus took too much out of him two days ago".

With this turn of events, James declared that he would be retiring from the hammer for good. It was something that he had been considering for some time. This only pushed him over the edge to confirm the decision. It was a decision that was supported even by his hammer coach Dr. Lothar Hinz, who agreed that specialising in the discus was the way to go.

Chapter 20

Recriminations

The dismal showing of Singapore athletics at the Brunei Games marked a nadir for the sport that had been in slow decline since the 1980s. The only gold and silver medals won at the Games out of the four participating Singaporeans were all attributed to James Wong. In *The Straits Times*' own published report card of the various sports' performance at the SEA Games, athletics was graded at "F". Furious at his under-performing athletes, President Loh Lin Kok lashed out at them in the media.

Even James was not spared when President Loh branded him a "failure" for losing the hammer gold. In one of his most infamous tirades to the press, he ranted with trademark vitriol that "either [James'] head is too big to contain his brain or he lacks the fighting spirit to rise to the occasion".

His stinging attack was a most curious way to treat a SEA Games champion and record holder who had been the sole provider of

Singapore athletics' SEA Games gold medals over 15 years. Showing uncharacteristic restraint, James refused to respond to President Loh's comments directly. Instead, he declared that he would no longer work with the Singapore Amateur Athletics Association (SAAA), and that he would only share his plans with the Singapore Sports Council (SSC) and seek their help to support him directly, bypassing the SAAA. This was a move that only served to further infuriate the athletics officials.

The drama would not end there, however, for both the SAAA and James.

The sorry state of Singapore athletics caused the sport to be dropped from the SSC's list of "core sports". This had dire financial implications since sports on the list were supported with up to 1 million dollars' worth of funding.

In April 2000, news broke that the SAAA had not nominated James for the Singapore National Olympic Council's (SNOC's) Meritorious Awards for its upcoming Singapore Sports Awards ceremony. The SAAA stated that, while James had met the criteria for nomination, he was found lacking in terms of attitude and discipline.

The SAAA went on to cite a long list of infractions that their star athlete had allegedly committed. For example, he demonstrated a prima donna attitude by insisting on being put up at The Sea View Hotel at the SAAA's expense, rather than staying in his own home on his return to Singapore before the SEA Games. He also refused to train at the SAAA's newly established Centre of Excellence at the

PART FOUR  The Tribe

Serangoon Stadium. The final straw was his act of bypassing the SAAA to seek support directly from the SSC.

James was naturally disappointed with this decision, believing he had done more than enough to warrant a nomination. Hoping to appeal directly to the SNOC, he was told that they could only select athletes that the SAAA had nominated. In frustration, James sent a lengthy email to *The Straits Times* protesting his treatment.

He would go on to defend himself publicly.

"I wanted to stay at The Sea View because it was much closer to the National Stadium where I was training. This has been a recurring arrangement with the SAAA ever since I started training overseas. If they had an issue with it, why did they approve it all those years ago and why only raise it now? As to why I didn't train at Serangoon, the facilities and weight room there were inadequate for my needs. All the equipment I needed could be found at the National Stadium. If they wanted me to perform and do well, surely I needed access to the best facilities. I bypassed the SAAA because I didn't think that the officials there really valued what I had done for them. Even after the SEA Games when I broke the discus record, I did not receive so much as a congratulatory note from anyone there. All they gave me was a trashing in the media for missing out on the hammer gold."

The tension was somewhat eased when the SAAA caved by submitting a last-minute nomination for James, even going as far as to nominate him for the Sydney Olympics happening later in the year. The SNOC duly approved his award nomination and he finally received his Meritorious Award for his contributions to Singapore sport.

Just days before the awards ceremony, James delivered a shocking statement declaring his intention to quit the sport. He expressed his profound disappointment at being doubted and treated in this manner despite winning a gold medal and breaking the SEA Games record. The SAAA promptly withdrew his Olympic nomination.

This move stunned the local sporting scene, with the SSC calling James' move "premature" in media statements. They believed that he still had a few more good sporting years left in him. After all, his national record set in 1999 ranked him as the top three discus throwers in Asia, raising hopes that he may yet challenge for a medal at the 2002 Busan Asian Games.

The SAAA placed a lid on the rumbling dispute with a final vindictive move. Through statements issued by both President Loh and Honorary Secretary Sarvindar Singh, they implied that James was only content to excel at the SEA Games level, casting doubts on his big match temperament to go beyond. It was a most ignominious and regrettable way to conclude the glittering season of an athlete who twice broke his national record and returned home from the SEA Games with a gold and silver medal, breaking the SEA Games record in the process.

"This was one of the most difficult periods of time for me. I'm not sure why a season which started off so promising ended in this way. I don't think I underperformed at all, and till this day, I do not

PART FOUR  The Tribe

understand the SAAA's criticism of me. I was their best athlete by a mile. It was most unfortunate that despite breaking the SEA Games record in the discus, they could not see beyond my hammer result. It really made me feel devalued after all I've given the sport. I'm not sure that was the best way to encourage athletes at a time when the sport needed fresh ideas."

While the denunciation by the SAAA did play a big part in James' decision to call time on his career, there were other personal considerations that contributed as well.

His German training stint had come to a natural conclusion at the end of 1999 and it was time to think about his future.

"I was already 31 at that point in my life. Other than being a professional athlete, I'd not held a full-time job. I had minimal CPF and had not seen an increase to my athlete salary for three years since I first went to Germany. I could not continue indefinitely like this. Sport was important to me, but so was my livelihood. I had sacrificed my best years for the sport and the financial remuneration I had received so far was far from adequate to push me to continue."

Family also strongly figured into his considerations. His relationship with Jana had progressed to a point where they were discussing a life together. She was also happy to move to Singapore to undertake the rest of the journey in their relationship.

Jana reflected on her decision to move at that point in time.

"My sporting career was pretty much over due to injuries at that point. Just before my move, I had to undergo surgery to fix a slip disc problem. This effectively ended any hopes I had of being competitive. It was time to also think about the next step in my life.

"Moving to Singapore had some risks for sure. But apart from wanting to start a family with James, I liked Singapore. The weather was warm and I loved the food. James' family was always welcoming to me, even if I couldn't always communicate clearly with his parents. Ultimately, I was committed to my decision to move, so much so that I shifted all my things over from Germany, all 1.2 tonnes of it!"

James and Jana ready to start their new life together. She moved to Singapore to be with her new husband.

PART FOUR  The Tribe

Using the savings he had amassed from the Major Games Award Programme and years of striking gold at the SEA Games, James was able to put a down payment for a flat in Mountbatten, just a stone's throw from his stomping ground, the Kallang National Stadium. He was now in need of stable income to help build his family nest.

This pushed him to seek full-time employment with the SSC as its strength and conditioning coach. Apart from managing the high-performance gym at the SSC, he was also responsible for planning and assisting with the strength-training needs of national athletes from across all sports.

These events closed one of the most significant chapters in the life and career of Southeast Asia's discus king. When he started out the year breaking national records in Germany, he certainly had no idea how life would take a turn for him, forcing him to seek greener pastures away from the familiar comforts of his sporting ecosystem. The sporting life was all he had known since he was a teenager. Now the equally exciting prospect of starting his own family led him to tread on paths previously unknown to him. Even so, as ever the consummate sportsman, it was a challenge he took head on with enthusiasm.

· Part Five ·

Will He, Won't He?

Chapter 21

The Road to Recovery

March 2023

Following a successful surgery, James was not out of the woods yet. During the operation, the doctors had removed the tumour with surrounding organs and lymph nodes as a whole and had sent them for a biopsy. This was done to determine that the cancer had not spread to these surrounding areas.

To his relief, the biopsy results revealed the tumour to be completely removed with clear margins, and no lymph nodes were involved with cancer. He was cancer-free. Now he had to take his first steps on the long hard road to recovery.

Although out of the hospital, James still experienced much of the post-surgery discomfort and side effects. There was soreness from his surgical wound, and he was constantly feeling bloated and fatigued. While he was slowly regaining his appetite, his stomach had shrunk from the surgery and he could only consume food in small portions. This in turn affected his energy levels. He also

PART FIVE  Will He, Won't He?

experienced cramps and tightness in his muscles. He was keen to pick up on his pre-surgery exercise routine, but that would have to wait for now.

It took some time for him to accept his current predicament; to live with these challenges on a daily basis which represented a new normal for him in a sense. But his athlete instincts soon took over. Not satisfied with the status quo, he began to push and probe at the limits of his capabilities, intending to overcome his challenges and take back his life.

There were encouraging signs. Within weeks, James was back to tucking into his favourite dishes like curry, *nasi lemak*, and *char kway teow*, although in smaller amounts. It was a rebound that stunned his family, especially since his digestive system was most certainly affected by the surgery.

Fitness-wise, he started with baby steps. He managed to improve his walking speed from 22 minutes per kilometre, which he clocked about a week after his discharge, to an impressive 15 after a month. At this speed, he could last for at most half an hour before calling it quits, but it felt great to stretch his legs again.

Soon, it was a trip back to the doctors. Given his recovery process, James would now have to meet with the oncologist from the National Cancer Centre Singapore at Changi General Hospital to discuss his chemotherapy treatment. Chemotherapy is given in this context to prevent spread of microscopic cancer cells that may be traveling in the blood stream and potentially spread to other parts of the body. While it is targeted to attack cancerous cells, it can also affect normal cells, especially those that may share some characteristics with cancer cells, hence leading to potential side effects.

James had some initial concerns about the side effects. The doctor reassured him that the severity differed from patient to patient. There were certain factors like age and fitness that would determine how well a patient responded to chemotherapy. But side effects like nausea, diarrhoea, constipation, and fatigue were to be expected.

With that reassurance, James was quietly confident he could handle whatever the treatment would throw at him. He opted to start on 17 April, almost two months after his surgery.

The process would involve the consumption of capecitabine, or Xeloda, in pill form. This chemotherapy form was chosen over others since his cancer was at stage two and considered less serious.

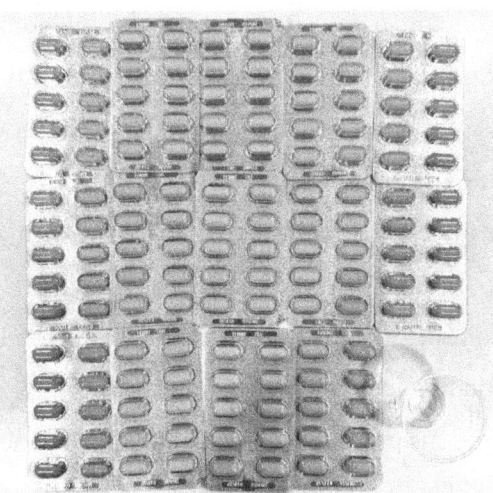

The quantity of Xeloda pills that James was required to consume in a single cycle of two weeks as part of his chemotherapy treatment.

PART FIVE  Will He, Won't He?

He would have to consume about five pills in the morning, and again in the evening daily. This dosage was above the norm due to his size and weight. The cycle would involve two weeks on medication, and one week off. This would be followed by a blood test to check his progress as well as if his body could handle the dosage. The whole process would take eight cycles, or six months, before it would be re-evaluated.

After a month or so, the side effects started to surface. James started to feel the bloatedness, gas, and some gag reflex after eating. His feet started to turn a darker shade of tan and black spots were appearing around the base of his feet and hands. His joints were also aching without a reason. Finally, his hair started to thin out from his head. However, he had mentally prepared himself for the worst and actually found these side effects manageable.

He was also eager to push the intensity of his exercise regime, but was cautioned by his doctors to take it slow, since the chemotherapy would have also weakened his body's resistance and immunity. With this in mind, he was mindful of receiving too many visitors which may have increased his risk of illness and infection.

After the first few cycles, the doctors felt confident with James' progress. All signs pointed to the fact that his side effects from chemotherapy were considered mild and that he was coping well with the treatment. The situation looked rosy for him.

Feeling satisfied with his progress, James enrolled in a pancreatic cancer support group. These sessions, that were facilitated by the

Singapore General Hospital and hosted by a retired doctor, enabled him to link up with patients at varying stages ranging from pre-surgery, post-surgery, to complete recovery. There, they shared stories of hope to encourage each other to stay strong and motivated.

"I was glad for these sessions. Meeting these people and listening to their stories, I found a lot of strength and encouragement. It provided some measure of comfort to know I wasn't alone in this. As an athlete, I was no stranger to fighting the odds, and to some extent, it helped to frame my struggle against cancer. But after hearing some of the stories shared at the support sessions, I was humbled to realise that my condition was mild compared to some of theirs. I suddenly felt fortunate that I was able to manage the symptoms better than some of the people I met. I also gained a healthy respect for these folks who were in worse shape than me, but still found the courage to confront their condition head on and share stories of encouragement. Some of these guys had more fight in them than athletes I know!

"It can also be disheartening sometimes to hear stories of relapses, especially happening to patients who were showing optimistic signs of recovery. It's unsettling to think that we might be like walking time bombs, poised for an unpredictable crisis.

"But there were positive stories as well. Just the other day, I met a gentleman who had his surgery a week before

PART FIVE  Will He, Won't He?

me, but was still suffering from severe post-surgery effects. I was able to share some tips to help him cope. I looked forward to these sessions because somehow, I had become a beacon of positivity to them. I felt upbeat and encouraged that in my given situation, I was still able to help others."

Jana was also able to sense her husband's newfound purpose in bringing hope to fellow cancer patients.

"I think it gave him a lot of satisfaction to be able to advise and bring cheer to people treading the same path as him. It really helped him snap out of the gloom that he was experiencing after his surgery."

Indeed, former teammates and colleagues of James could attest to the fact that he was often the life of the party. Now, he could use his outgoing personality to bring a message of hope and belief to an environment that was often bereft of it. It was a role he revelled in.

Chapter 22

"Is He Even Human?"

12 June 2001

Sports journalists representing the major media outlets were gathered in a function room at Nike's headquarters in Tampines. Excited chatter filled the room as the reporters speculated among one another as to why they were summoned. All they knew was that they had received an invite from Nike Singapore, who was acting on behalf of the reigning discus SEA Games champion and record holder James Wong. Nike had been supporting the local athletics star since 1996. The journalists were informed that James would be making a statement.

The conversations tapered off as the hulking thrower entered the room, flanked by his Nike representatives. Tapping the microphone set-up before him to test that it was working, he went straight to his announcements.

"At this weekend's SAAA All-Comers Meet, I will be competing in the discus event to try and qualify for the SEA Games at Kuala Lumpur in September.

PART FIVE  Will He, Won't He?

"I have been encouraged by my recent training performances as well as strong support from my employer (the SSC), my sponsor Nike as well as my wife Jana. I would like to also add that Jana and I are currently expecting our first child and she will be due sometime close to the SEA Games. We have already discussed and anticipated the possible scenarios in order to make this arrangement work. If I do get a medal, it will be dedicated to my wife and newborn daughter."

Immediately, questions fired across the room from every topic ranging from his training performances to his wife's pregnancy.

After answering the questions as best as he could, he ended the session with a teasing invite to the journalists who were curious as to whether he was still the same colossus who took the SEA Games by storm from 1993 to 1999.

"Come to Serangoon Stadium this weekend, you'll see for yourself."

While many stars had aligned for James to make this fateful decision, it still was not an easy one to make due to the drastic changes in lifestyle that he had to undergo since his decision to quit a year prior.

He now had to juggle full-time employment with training, something he never had to do before. Prior to this, he had taken up a few part-time coaching jobs, but ultimately had to settle for something full-time to facilitate Jana's application for Singapore permanent residency.

His new job as the Singapore Sports Council's (SSC's) new strength and conditioning coach also had its perks. His office was situated in a high-performance gym at the Kallang National Stadium, just next to the track and field. On a typical work day, he could cycle to work from his flat in Mountbatten, which was a mere 10-minute ride away, and start training at seven in the morning. After which, he would start work at about nine till noon, where he would break for lunch. Then his rest consisted of a quick ride home for an afternoon nap, before resuming his training at three. He would then receive the next batch of national athletes who would report at five and assist with their strength training until eight or nine in the evening.

Working at the National Stadium gym afforded James some balance between work and training.

PART FIVE  Will He, Won't He?

James also kept in touch with his former coach Gerhard Böttcher who helped him with his training planning as well as provided feedback for improvement.

It was a punishing work–training schedule, but he was determined to make it work. After all, the process was definitely smoothened by how his training facilities were lined up around him. Under his desk was a bag of discuses which he could pick and go for practice whenever it was time. He also had access to the biomechanics and sports science facilities at the stadium. His employers at the SSC were happy to offer their blessings and support for his training as long as it did not adversely affect his work.

His family arrangements were somewhat more complicated, however. Jana reflected on this decision that they took together: "I was an athlete. I understood the allure of competition and all the thrill that it brought. But as a first-time expectant mother in a foreign country, I hoped to have my husband by my side as well, especially with the delivery date looming. We talked about it a lot before we finally decided on the course that he took."

Together, they worked out contingency plans for every possible scenario they could anticipate. They had a plan for if the baby came before, during, and after the SEA Games. James contacted his sisters who agreed to be on standby and provide support just in case Jana delivered while he was away at Kuala Lumpur.

That Sunday on 17 June, crowds packed Serangoon Stadium in an expectant mood to see what James could produce. It was something of a novel experience to watch him compete as well. Although a Singaporean, his best results had always been achieved overseas and local athletics fans rarely got to see James in action at local stadiums.

His performance left his fans in awe as he delivered a 57.47-metre throw on his third attempt, dispelling any misguided notions that he was over the hill. A journalist even overheard a star-struck school boy exclaim in the stands, "Is he even human?"

It was a result that would have won any of the previous SEA Games editions prior to 1999. It also catapulted him to the status of clear favourite, since his closest rival Wansawang Sawasdee the Thai had barely crossed the 50-metre mark in his best attempt of the year so far.

He would reflect on his comeback decision years later. "I had so many conversations with Jana before I finally decided to take the plunge. I knew I could not do it without her support and blessings. I was just grateful she understood. We really felt like a team making this decision together. Yet, I also needed to fulfil my obligations now as a family man. It was just a delicate balance. But training was good, and I knew my rivals had not yet caught up. So I felt I was good enough for one more gold."

An interesting development that had also been brewing since 1999 was the introduction of six China-based throwers to the local athletics scene. Perhaps acutely aware of the Singapore Amateur Athletics Association's over-reliance on James for SEA Games gold medals, this was President Loh Lin Kok's attempt to add to the gold medal count

PART FIVE  Will He, Won't He?

and inject some much-needed impetus into the ailing sport.

After training in Singapore for two years, they had been officially unveiled to the public to much fanfare and controversy. While many commentators acknowledged that they would bring in the gold medals, some were sceptical of the scheme, since the China-based thrower would displace the local throwers and deny them of the opportunity to compete for Singapore. The biggest challenge for the China-based throwers at that moment, however, was to gain their citizenship papers so that they could represent the Republic at major competitions like the SEA Games.

For the 2001 SEA Games, the only athlete among the six to clear this hurdle was 20-year-old Dong Enxin, a male shot put specialist from Liaoning. He had already bettered the SEA Games shot put record when he recorded a 17.48-metre distance at the Philippines Open earlier in the year. At the Inter-Club Championships in August 2001, he swung the discus to 51.77 metres, making him the second best all-time discus thrower in Singapore, even if the event was not his pet event. It set up the tantalising possibility of a Singapore one-two finish in the event at the SEA Games the next month. In his first shot put competition as a Singapore citizen, Dong also erased James' shot put record by an eye-popping 2 metres with a 17.33-metre throw. He looked set to take the burden off James as Singapore's sole gold medal provider.

Chapter 23

One Night in Kuala Lumpur

During the lead up to the Games in September, James fell back on his tried and tested strategy of media silence on all discussions concerning his medal hopes.

"I prefer to do all my talking in the discus cage," he explained.

Despite the deafening silence, the media knew that the semi-retired athlete was still the overwhelming favourite for the gold. Even his rivals acknowledged it when a Thai coach remarked to the media that "in order for Wansawang to win, we would have to cut off one of James' legs".

It was a crude expression, but the point was well noted.

In a special dispensation afforded to James due to his family situation, the Singapore National Olympic Council and the Singapore Amateur Athletics Association (SAAA) allowed him to fly into Kuala Lumpur on the morning of the competition and return to Singapore

PART FIVE Will He, Won't He?

the next morning. Although it was a short flight and climate conditions were similar to Singapore, this was still a risk. Conventional high-performance wisdom usually required the athlete to arrive at least a day or two before the competition in order to be well-rested and acclimatised to the environment and surroundings. The acclimatisation period would be longer if there were drastic climate or time differences.

On the morning of 14 September, James said his goodbyes to his family, promising to bring home the gold medal for Jana and his soon-to-be-born daughter, whom the couple had decided to name Jessica. The flight took about an hour. From the airport, he was whisked to the team hotel just in time for lunch.

After a quick meal, he tried to take a nap, but found his thoughts racing.

"I thought of Jana back home, and wondered if Jessica would choose this moment to make her grand appearance. I also thought of the competition and wondered if I was taking things perhaps a bit too lightly by flying only on the day of the competition. These were all distractions and I could not rest."

After several failed attempts to nap, he decided to head down to the practice track early at three in the afternoon.

When he got there, he was dazzled by the majestic sight of the imposing Bukit Jalil National Stadium towering above the surrounding neighbourhood. The 88,000-capacity stadium was built to serve as Malaysia's centrepiece when it hosted the 1998 Commonwealth

Games. It was a competition that James would have attended if not for the wrist injury that had sidelined him that year. He thought it was the biggest stadium he ever saw. Nevertheless, he felt it poignant that he would now compete at this stadium to make up for his previous lost opportunity.

A heavy downpour just before the event made conditions in the stadium hot and humid, especially for James who was soaked in sweat inside his Nike bodysuit. It was also his first time competing at night under the trained glare of floodlights that not only illuminated the entire field of play, but also the residual moisture dotting the damp evening air. Yet, the conditions did little to slow his unstoppable march to victory which was already decided by the first throw. His final result was 56.98 metres recorded on his third attempt.

Compatriot Dong Enxin, who was hyped for the silver, succumbed to nerves, successfully completing only three out of his six attempts. He lost the silver to Wansawang Sawasdee, who by now was getting accustomed to this medal colour whenever he had to compete against James.

The younger Singaporean was so nervous at one point that James stepped in to guide him with some pointers to improve his subsequent throws. It was a heart-warming display of sportsmanship from the elder statesman in his first competition with his younger challenger.

This result only added to Dong's earlier disappointment for missing out on the shot put gold after he was tipped to break the record. He had to settle for silver, losing by 20 centimetres to Thai Chatchawal

PART FIVE  Will He, Won't He?

Polyemg who broke the Games' record.

With the gold in the bag and mission accomplished, James only returned to the hotel close to midnight after going through doping control. The next morning, he was on the first flight back to Singapore. All in all, he spent a grand total of 24 hours in the Malaysian capital, which was just enough time for him to win his fifth consecutive discus crown.

"There were a lot of comments about how easy I made it look, to be in and out of KL in 24 hours and back with the gold medal. But what these commentators failed to see were the struggles I had with work, training and family, the 15-hour work/training days I put in for months just so that I could get ready for the Games. This was a special result for me, my first gold since I started a full-time job and as a family man. I was so happy I could win it for my wife and Jessica."

In the end, everything worked out nicely for James. He got his gold, returned to his wife, and Jessica was born a month later in October.

James' latest victory once again put him in contention for the two biggest competitions on 2002's calendar: the Asian and Commonwealth Games.

The SAAA was also keen to make amends with their SEA Games hero of the past decade with President Loh Lin Kok commenting to *The Straits Times* that "James did us proud again". They also reached out to him to discuss his plans for the future.

However, he put a damper on these ideas by declaring that he was now a "family man".

"My priorities are now different with Jana and Jessica in my life. I had not trained since I came back from Kuala Lumpur. Jana and I were also still adjusting to keeping odd hours so that Jessica could be fed. We even had to get a helper to assist us. I really did not give much thought to competing again. I also had a job which I loved and wanted to excel in. Athletics was really the last thing on my mind. Although I did not officially declare it, there was a possibility that I could have walked away from the sport once more at this point given my shifting priorities."

It seemed that he had retired once more.

There were also other developments in the athletics scene that paved the way for a thaw in the frosty relations between James and the SAAA. As part of a leadership renewal process, Loh Lin Kok announced that he would relinquish his presidency in 2004 to oil trader Tang Weng Fei, who was also chairman of S-League club Woodlands Wellington. Tang, a former national hurdler himself, would understudy the veteran sports administrator as vice-president until he was ready to assume the hot seat. There were also plans to rebrand the association as the Singapore Athletics Association, or SAA, to reflect a more professional approach towards managing the sport and its athletes.

All these were part of an overall strategy to improve relations with

PART FIVE  Will He, Won't He?

the Singapore Sports Council that were also strained due to years of clashes between Loh and the sports governing authority. This was coupled with improved results at the SEA Games with new faces like U. K. Shyam and Dong Enxin leading the charge. There was a sense that athletics would finally rise from the ashes once more. The question was whether James would be a part of this future.

Chapter 24

A Lap of Honour

On a sunny May afternoon in 2003, James stood in his favourite discus ring at the Kallang National Stadium, launching discus after discus towards the opposite end of the field. After exhausting his supply, he would trudge slowly across to gather them for the next round of throws. It seemed routine, except the ring was surrounded by journalists who were documenting his every move during training.

It was now official: after months of speculation, the discus king would return to defend his SEA Games title in 2003, held for the first time in the Vietnamese capital of Hanoi.

"It was a carefully considered decision. Our family had achieved some level of stability and we were able to cope better with what was happening at home. I surveyed the regional field and those guys weren't getting any better as well. I knew I could still put in a strong challenge. My daughter already has a Games mascot from KL, I would very much like to win one for my son."

PART FIVE   Will He, Won't He?

James at the "Grand Old Dame", the nickname for the former National Stadium. The stadium including the nearby Kallang Practice Track held many special memories for him. It was where he was first introduced to the sport, where he broke countless age-group records, the site of his first SEA Games victory, and later became his work and training ground.

Indeed, young Jordan Wong would be due in September that year, before the SEA Games in December. James and Jana were now more experienced and better equipped to manage a second child.

However, there were still challenges for Jana.

"Single parenting was not easy at all. I was more experienced this time, but to have two little kids running around the house crying for attention was not always the easiest thing at times. There was one day when Jessica wouldn't stop crying and I got so exasperated. Even bringing her to the clinic didn't help, as the doctor couldn't figure out what was happening. But the moment James walked through the front door after getting home from work, she started smiling again. I just couldn't figure

Shifting priorities. James made it clear at this point that his family would take priority for him. In the picture, Jana is holding baby Jordan while James is with young Jessica.

out what had just happened, but seeing my little girl chuckling away in his huge arms was such a relief for me. While I understood his decision to compete, it really helped when he was around."

To add to Team Singapore's excitement, two more naturalised citizens would be joining the expanding throw contingent at the year-end games when shot putters Zhang Guirong and Du Xianhui received their citizenship papers and the green light to compete. Both athletes were in top form and good bets for gold. They joined James and Dong Enxin to make a party of four.

"It was an interesting situation," James reflected. "For as far as I could remember in my career, the sprinters always got the limelight.

PART FIVE  Will He, Won't He?

For once, we had so many throwers who were going to make a real difference to Singapore athletics' medal tally, and it was exciting to see the focus on us for once."

To add to James' spotlight at the SEA Games that December, and perhaps also as recognition of his standing in Singapore sports, he was selected by a panel at the Singapore National Olympic Council to be the nation's flag bearer at the opening ceremony of the Games. While it was a great honour for the veteran athlete, it also added to his pressure.

In his words: "The flag bearer is always expected to win the gold."

Already towering at 1.90 metres, the Singaporean giant rallied his nation's contingent and ensured that the crescent moon and stars flew high and proud on a cold winter's evening at Hanoi's My Dinh Stadium, built specially for this Games. The opening ceremony was a historic moment for Vietnam, and a special one for James Wong.

The discus event was scheduled on the first day of the athletics competition and he could not have been prepared for what he witnessed. The stadium was packed with 40,000 screaming fans chanting and cheering during every moment they thought was significant. There were also cheerleaders strategically dispersed among the crowd to lead the spectators on.

"It was amazing! I only ever witnessed such scenes at football games, and I was usually in the stands. But to have the crowd cheering

Team Singapore's SEA Games 2003 contingent in Hanoi was led by James (right of picture with the flag) during the Games' opening ceremony.

the athletes was special. I'm not sure if they even knew what they were cheering for, but it didn't matter to me. It really fired me up and I was more determined than ever to win."

The competition was far from routine, however, as the perennial discus bridesmaid Wansawang Sawasdee stunningly opened with 54.80 metres, smashing his own Thai national record and rattling James' unflappable composure. Even though the veteran was still in the lead with his first attempt of 55 metres, he knew full well that his younger Thai rival was closing the gap. No other Southeast Asian except for James had thrown further than 53 metres at the SEA Games; this challenge became too close for comfort for the defending champion.

PART FIVE Will He, Won't He?

Emboldened by the cheering Vietnamese crowd, James launched into an impromptu lap of honour after his discus victory with the national flag.

He managed to put some distance between the challenger and himself with 56.49 metres while Wansawang was snapping at his heels all the way. Finally, the Thai thrower stepped up for his final attempt and chance to dethrone the king. As he released the discus, it sliced through the air at a steady trajectory, landing beyond the 55-metre distance marker. It was a new national record for the Thai, but would it be enough for the gold medal? James held his breath in nervous anticipation while the measurement was taken. The winter cool air in the stadium did nothing to calm his nerves as his hands, which were tightly clasped together, froze into numbness.

"55.71 metres" read the electronic scoreboard after what felt like hours for the anxious throwers.

James jumped in the air and punched his fists in triumph. He had snatched yet another victory, albeit by a margin that was much closer than he would have liked.

With the adrenaline from the intense competition still throbbing in his veins and the incessant chanting of the boisterous crowd echoing all around him, he spontaneously reached for the Singapore flag in his bag and broke into a jog, holding it aloft and fluttering over his shoulders in a lap of honour.

"I have never done a lap of honour in all my victories, but seeing the cheering crowd really fired me up. So I thought to myself 'Heck it, let's do this!' When I reached the opposite end of the stadium, I saw at the shot put pit that Du Xianhui had also won the shot put event. I recognised the significance of the moment for us throwers

PART FIVE Will He, Won't He?

Both James and Du Xianhui had won their gold medals at around the same time in the stadium and shared a joint lap of honour to celebrate this momentous occasion for Singapore. This was the first time that another Singaporean other than James had struck gold in athletics at the SEA Games since 1983.

and invited her to join me in completing my lap."

Indeed, 21-year-old Du had emerged victorious at her maiden SEA Games by smashing the shot put record at 18.20 metres. Her fellow teammate Zhang Guirong had also finished as runner-up to complete a one-two finish for Singapore.

The crowd and the organisers were happy to indulge the victorious duo seeing how they had entertained the stadium, to the extent that all track events were placed on hold until the throwers had finished their celebrations. The enduring image of both Du and James holding up the Singapore flag in a joint celebration became symbolic of a turning point for Singapore athletics. This represented the first occasion since 1983 when a Singaporean not named James Wong won an athletics gold medal at the SEA Games. No longer would he bear the sole burden of providing gold medals for his nation.

All in all, the four throwers reaped a bumper harvest at the Games as they plundered a total of four gold and three silver medals for Singapore. Zhang and Du repeated their one-two finish in the women's discus with Zhang edging out her teammate this time. Zhang also participated in the javelin event, finishing second. Dong Enxin, who had a disappointing debut in 2001, rebounded spectacularly by striking gold at the shot put event.

James recalled the 2003 Hanoi Games with much fondness. "I had a scare in the discus and perhaps underestimated Wansawang's improvement from the last Games. It had been a long time since a competitor pushed me this hard in the event. Ultimately, I managed to win my sixth discus gold, the crowd was fantastic, and it was a solid outing for Singapore throwers and athletes. This was a memorable SEA Games for me."

The year following the Hanoi Games in 2004 proved to be a year of honours and affirmation for the veteran athlete.

After receiving the Meritorious Award at the Singapore Sports Awards on five previous occasions, the thrower finally clinched the top award, Sportsman of the Year, for the first time in his

The Singapore "friendly giant" celebrating yet another SEA Games victory, his sixth in the discus while Wansawang Sawasdee (left in picture) looks on.

Crowned as Sportsman of the Year at the Singapore Sports Awards in 2004, James received his honour from then Prime Minister Goh Chok Tong.

storied career. He was 35 years of age at this time. He would be the first athletics representative in 30 years to win this award since high jumper Noor Azhar Hamid received this honour back in 1973. President Loh Lin Kok was quick to laud his star athlete by hailing his "consistency".

James would add to his list of honours when he was conferred the Singapore Youth Award in the Sports and Adventure category. Apart from his sporting achievements, the panel also looked favourably on his role in supporting para-athletes on a volunteer basis with his strength training expertise.

PART FIVE  Will He, Won't He?

The icing on the cake that was a year filled with honours came when he was named as one of the Singaporean torch bearers to represent the nation at the Olympic Torch Relay held in Greece. The 2004 Olympics would return to its spiritual birthplace that year when Athens was named as its host city. He would join a multi-national contingent numbering close to 11,000 athletes participating in the relay. His running leg was situated on the Greek island of Crete, famous for the half-man half-bull Minotaur of Greek mythology. He would run a total of 200 metres near the Cave of Diktaion Andron, also known as the birthplace of the Greek God Zeus. After that, he would pass the torch to fellow Singaporean and adventurer Khoo Swee Chiow.

James described his experience as "magical". It was also a consolation for him after narrowly missing out on the Olympics back in 1996. To remember and commemorate this special moment, James brought back his own Olympic torch and donated it to the Singapore Sports Museum where it is still on display at the time of this book's writing.

A Lap of Honour

A belated Olympic moment. James at the Olympic torch relay in Greece.

Chapter 25

The "Thrilla in Manila"

Unlike the uncertainty that characterised his participation in the previous two SEA Games, James demonstrated a stronger resolve to compete in the Manila edition in 2005.

"I knew Wansawang was catching up. But I still felt good and knew that I had it in me to win the gold again. My kids were also slightly older now, which gave me a greater peace of mind to train and compete."

After routinely qualifying for the Games at the Fifth All-Comers Meet when he threw 55 metres, he was set for a showdown with his Thai rival, until circumstances took a different turn for him.

During a family lunch at home in September, Jana suddenly fainted and had to be rushed to the hospital. The family then found out that she had contracted dengue fever and was hospitalised for five days. It was around that time that health authorities had warned that dengue cases were on the rise. James knew about the warnings, but never expected that he would be struck down as well barely two weeks after his wife's hospitalisation.

He described the experience as "two weeks of hell. I would break out in cold sweats and my body was shivering constantly. My temperature was 39.7 degrees at one point. I felt too weak to even stand and was lying in bed most of the time. My body basically shut down during those weeks. By the time I started to get better, my muscle mass had shrunk dramatically and I had lost almost 10 kilograms. My Adidas competition suit that used to fit snugly on me suddenly felt loose. I knew I was in trouble."

When he recovered and finally mustered enough strength to take to the training field again, James realised the magnitude of the problem that was confronting him.

"For the first couple of training sessions, none of my throws went beyond 50 metres. It was already October when I started training again and the SEA Games was in December. A full training cycle would take about six to eight months. I had six weeks. I was basically starting back at zero and it frustrated me. The thought that I might not win did cross my mind. It made me angry, not because I could lose to a stronger rival, but because I wasn't in my best form to compete."

In a surreal experience for James, he did not arrive in Manila as the clear favourite. Wansawang Sawasdee had been averaging 55–56 metres from his training stint in Beijing. The best James could manage was 53 metres two weeks before the Games. To turn up the

PART FIVE  Will He, Won't He?

heat on the defending champion, the Thais had a new up and coming youngster Kvanchai Numsomboon who had broken the 50-metre mark as well.

Manila also did not hold happy memories for James. The last time he competed at the SEA Games hosted there in 1991, he finished without a medal, the one and only time in his career that that had happened. His head was filled with pessimistic thoughts that he had to fight to keep at bay. He was at the SEA Games representing his nation, and he knew he had to put up a good show.

His loss of form could not have come at a worse time.

Despite his setbacks, the veteran's experience showed. He surged to an early lead with 52.31 metres to Wansawang's 50.65 metres. At the fifth throw, the Thai dug deep to hurl 52.51 metres, taking a slim 20-centimetre lead. It was the first time in his life that he had done so against James. He was elated, and so was the Thai camp. James was shell-shocked. This was unfamiliar territory for both men.

At his prime, having to produce strong performances on his fifth or sixth attempt would not have been much of a problem. However, the ageing war horse was far from his physical prime, especially having suffered from the ravages of dengue only two months before.

He composed himself mentally, knowing it was a do-or-die situation. If he had anything left in the tank, it had to be given in the fifth attempt. He knew he could not last till the sixth.

The hallmark of a true champion is the ability to summon game-winning performances when one's back is against the wall. In this

After rebounding from a serious bout of dengue fever in 2005, James had to fend off a determined challenge from the fast-improving Thais in his weakened state.

PART FIVE Will He, Won't He?

regard, James demonstrated why he was a six-time winner in this event. Channelling all his inner strength, he let loose a stunner that saw the discus land at 55.11 metres. It was a huge attempt — his best since his brush with dengue. He was back in the lead again in the most emphatic fashion. He sank back into his chair at the rest area, knowing he had nothing left to give. Over to Wansawang.

The Thai stepped up for his final throw, his last chance to take the crown that had cruelly evaded his grasp on so many occasions. The Thai officials were all at the edge of their seats to see if their challenger could win a historic gold.

James could not bear to look. He was seated with his head buried in his hands in nervous apprehension. His hands were quivering from a mixed bag of excitement, exhaustion, and nerves. He could feel his heartbeat racing and pulsing through the nerve endings of his fingers. He was physically and mentally spent. If Wansawang had delivered here, this was it. His six-gold streak would come to an unceremonious end at the Rizal Memorial Stadium, the very same site of his heartbreak in 1991 when he was sent home without so much as a medal to his name.

The tension in the air was pierced by a shrill, metallic clanging noise. James knew this sound well. He looked up at that moment and saw the Thai's discus rolling harmlessly around the pit. It never touched the turf. His discus had smashed against the safety cage that surrounded the pit.

James leapt to his feet, raising his arms in victory. Number seven

Seven discus golds and counting. With his back against the wall, James managed to summon a gold-medal performance in his final throw to keep his discus streak going.

PART FIVE  Will He, Won't He?

was secured. He immediately waived off his sixth attempt, knowing that it would not have mattered anyway.

As journalists swarmed around him after the competition, the enormity of the occasion finally shattered his emotional dam. He erupted into sobs struggling to translate his thoughts into coherent words, often taking pauses to wipe his tears with a towel.

He tried to make light of his situation to the gathered reporters, who were surely bemused to see the 1.90-metre giant in tears. "I can't remember when the last time I cried was. Perhaps in '93 when I first won."

Placing his fingers to his temple, he remarked, "This is where it counts in the end. I had to fight back from zero after my illness. To all my challengers, it takes more than that to beat me. This medal is for my family who has been through so much in the last six weeks."

In a scene reminiscent of the *Rocky* films he grew up watching in the 1980s, he called Jana with a borrowed phone after the interview and yelled, "I did it!"

He recalled much later, "I was under so much pressure. Obviously everyone was expecting the gold. But I couldn't publicly admit that my confidence had taken a hit especially when the illness had reset all my training gains. The victory triggered a release in emotions that I had been holding back during those difficult weeks."

In a post-event interview with *Today*, the usually soft-spoken Wansawang also let loose emotions of his own, frustrated at playing second fiddle to the Singaporean yet again. "I'm getting sick of James.

He has beaten me every time since 1995. Every two years I try to beat him but I can't."

As an interesting footnote to an eventful SEA Games, it is worth mentioning that James also took part in the shot put event. At the technical meeting, the Singapore Athletics Association officials realised that there were only two competitors in the event, and signing James up would not only help the team's medal count (since he was assured of a bronze), but also allow the event to take place since the technical rules stated that it could not carry on with just two throwers. Defending champion Dong Enxin was unfortunately sidelined with a torn chest muscle and missed the Games.

There would be no fairy tale ending for James as he could do little against seasoned shot putters. He ended up with a bronze medal as expected.

James spent much of the years since setting the SEA Games record in Brunei in 1999 teasing the general public about his intentions to compete and continue. It was in fact nothing short of amazing that he continued his gold medal winning streak while juggling a full-time job and serving as a family man to his wife and two young children. He has often been open with the fact that his family's support meant everything to him, both throughout his career as well as with a different struggle years after he retired.

PART SIX Setbacks...

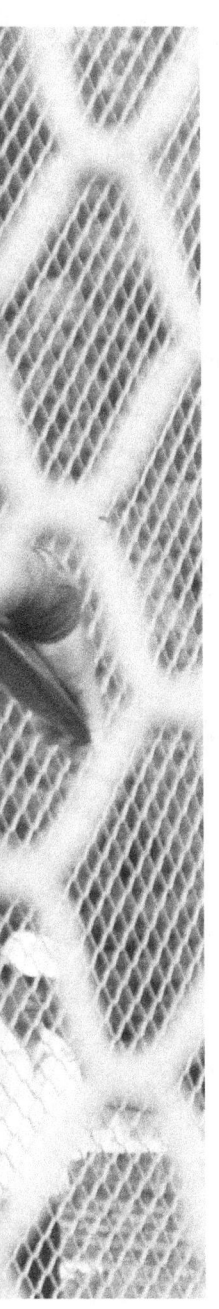

Chapter 26

Not Again

26 June 2023

James was tossing and turning in bed in the early hours of a June morning. He was trying his best to sleep, but an unbearable pain in his abdomen prevented him from doing so. Try as he might, he could not find a suitable position that could offer him any semblance of relief. He was frustrated and worried all at the same time.

The next morning, he tried to go about his day as normal. However, every time he tried to eat, he would end up throwing up. He could not pass motion the entire day as well.

He immediately took time off to see a general practitioner at a nearby clinic. The doctor prescribed some medicine for diarrhoea and told him to visit the hospital if things did not get better.

PART SIX  Setbacks...

There was no discernible improvement the next day. Finally on 28 June, he contacted CGH and an appointment for scheduled for him at the next available opportunity at the clinic that same morning.

He reached the hospital first thing in the morning at eight, and was immediately directed to take an X-ray. The resultant image indicated a bulge in his small intestines. The doctor was not able to diagnose it immediately and asked to take a closer look. James was directed to take a CT scan later that morning, and to return after lunch for the results and follow up.

There, he was told to his dismay that his small intestines were swollen due to adhesions, which are points in the intestine where they are blocked as a result of scar tissue, causing intestinal obstruction. With any abdominal surgery, there is always a risk that scar tissue can form any time and cause blockage of the intestines. In James' case, this occurred many months after he had fully recovered from his initial operation. While surgeries are not usually required in such situations, an operation may be necessary in severe cases or after a complex operation to relieve the blockage.

"Looks like we'll have to go into emergency surgery to sort this out," Dr. Chiow told him in a matter-of-fact manner. "We may have a window this evening to operate and get a closer look, maybe sort things out before they get worse."

The speed of these developments threw James off. He was overwhelmed and startled all at the same time.

"My first reaction was 'not again'. I was still reeling from the effects of the previous surgery and now I had to go back for another one, and it was scheduled for that very evening. But once I got over the initial shock, I knew it had to be done and I had no other options. The pain was really uncomfortable and this was the only way they could resolve it. I knew the surgery wouldn't be as major as my previous one, but it still soured my mood."

That day also happened to be Jana's birthday. The celebrations would have to wait.

James was admitted at five in the evening and whisked away to surgery at six. By now, he was a seasoned veteran of surgeries and it helped to calm his anxiety.

Perhaps as a way to challenge himself, he wilfully attempted to resist the anaesthetic gas administered through a breathing mask, just to see how long he could last. It did not make much of a difference before he blacked out again.

The laparotomy surgery took about two hours before James was roused at around nine in the evening. He learnt that the doctors managed to clean and untwist his small intestines back to their original state. This was the preferred outcome as compared to the other pre-surgery option that was presented to him: in the worst-case scenario, the doctors would have had to remove part of the intestine and reattach it together.

The recovery process this time round was also smoother. James had been through this before. He knew how to manage his own reaction to pain and was certainly wiser for it.

PART SIX Setbacks...

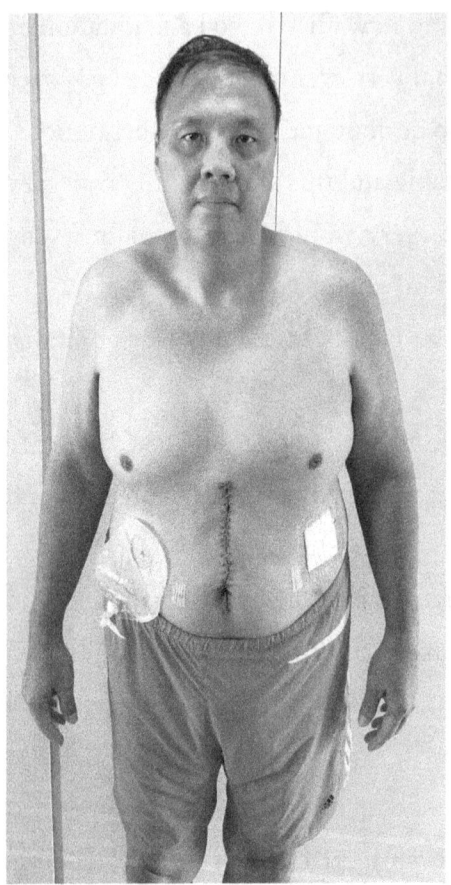
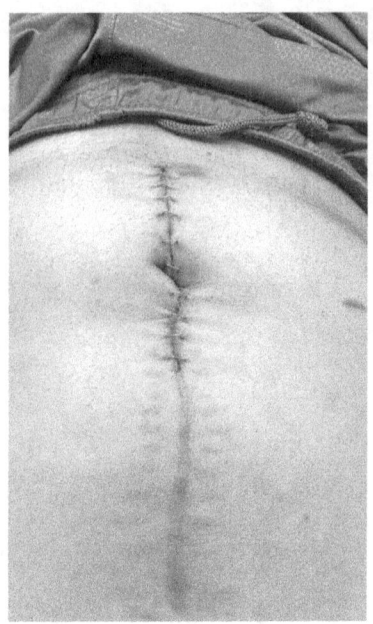

James' surgical scar after his first (left) and second (above) operation. After his second surgery, his scar now noticeably extends below his navel.

"As usual, the pain was there. I refused to self-administer any painkillers to help my body adjust to the recovery. I knew the discomfort would get better with each day, and I didn't want to become dependent on medication to manage it. I now had an extended surgery scar as well. I was also placed on a liquid diet for the first five days to allow my intestines time to recover. This caused my weight to drop to 105 kilograms. Mobility-wise, I was definitely more mobile this time, better able to manage simple tasks like going to the toilet myself after three days."

After the fifth day, he was able to take solid food and pass motion, a clear sign that the blockage in his intestinal system had been cleared. This paved the way for his discharge after a week on 3 July to recuperate at home.

"This setback was indeed frustrating for me. But I saw it as a detour on my long road to recovery. I was still moving in the right direction, slowly but surely. I had weathered a lot of challenges to get to where I was at that point, I was not about to give up. These things happen in life as they do in sports, we have no choice but to keep pushing onwards. That's where the positive results will come."

Chapter 27

The Last Train to the Asiad

January 2006

Shortly after his victory in Manila, a debate emerged concerning how long James could keep this gold medal streak going. The Thais were improving at each subsequent Games. He conceded that while there were a few promising throwers, an immediate successor was nowhere in sight and certainly would not be ready for 2007. James even made an offer through the media to coach any aspiring thrower who wanted to continue his legacy.

But for the moment, he was fully focused on making it to the 2006 Asiad held in Doha. After a glittering career at the SEA Games, it ate at him that he had not yet tested himself against the best in the continent, having once been ranked top three.

He was in a confident mood. "I had already thrown 55 metres under trying conditions. With more focus and consistency in my training, I was confident of meeting the qualifying mark of 57.78 metres."

Knowing full well this was likely his final shot at the Asiad, James threw himself back into the grind. Part of this even involved a trip back to his old training ground in Halle, Germany, where he reconnected with his former coach Gerhard Böttcher for a month-long training stint with competitions lined up to help him qualify.

Using his connections with senior Thai athletics officials, James was also able to arrange for a training stint at Thammasat University just outside of Bangkok, which was the training base for the Thai athletics team.

The Thai set-up was something that left an indelible impression on him.

"The training and dormitory facilities were basic, but like Germany, it was a training centre dedicated solely to athletics. However, it was the attention to detail and coherence in training development that really stood out for me. From youth level, the Thais were groomed carefully in developmental phases all the way to senior elite level where they were ready to perform for Thailand at the international stage. You got the sense that from the youth to the senior coaches, there was one coherent plan with common developmental milestones that every coach adhered to. It was a well-oiled production line that helped the Thais churn out talents and clearly demonstrated why they were 'kings of Southeast Asian athletics'. I only wish we had something like this in Singapore, where

PART SIX  Setbacks...

talent identification and development seemed to happen more by chance than by systemic planning."

Training in Thailand also allowed James to rekindle the old feeling of a professional full-time athlete once more, something which gave him more focus. In his downtime, he would hang out with the local Thai athletes like Wansawang Sawasdee, the Thai thrower who often played second fiddle to him.

In Germany, James managed to recapture a glimpse of his previous form when he recorded 56.05 metres at a competition. However, it was still more than a metre short of the 57.78-metre distance that the Singapore National Olympic Council (SNOC) had set as the qualifying mark. To his disappointment, his name did not appear in the initial list of 114 athletes going to Doha that was published in July.

A lifeline was handed to the thrower when he was given two more opportunities at the Singapore and Malaysia Open meets in September to qualify under appeal. However, he fell short once again, his best attempt out of the two meets being 53.21 metres. Given his distance to the qualifying mark, the Singapore Athletics Association (SAA) made a decision not to submit an appeal for him.

To his great annoyance, the thrower declared that he would quit and not contest the 2007 SEA Games.

"I had thrown 56 metres that year and would have improved further given time. The Asian Games was held in December and there was still some time to put in work and improve on my distances. I had always delivered for the SAA and I was disappointed they did not even see fit to raise an appeal. I would have understood if they had appealed and the SNOC rejected it. But to withdraw my name from consideration entirely was a clear sign of the lack of faith they had in me. Since they no longer believed in me, I didn't see the need to stick my neck out for them to train for 2007 as well."

It was at this time that James had also decided to join a team led by former SAA vice-president Steven Lee that was challenging President Loh Lin Kok's management team for the SAA elections in 2006.

"Given my exposure to regional and international high-performance systems, I felt that the current SAA team was lacking in terms of viable ideas and plans to move us forward. My recent training stints in Germany and Thailand only reinforced these perceptions. Many local athletes apart from myself also had gripes with the SAA's management. If they didn't even see fit to support a multiple SEA Games gold medallist like me, I was not sure what they could have done for other athletes who were struggling."

Ultimately, the challenge came to nothing when the SAA's affiliates gave a clear mandate to Loh's team at the SAA's 2006 Annual General Meeting for another two-year term. However, James' desire to see change would not be extinguished. The embers continued to glow in his heart as he awaited another moment when he could contribute to the sport in a meaningful way.

Chapter 28

"Thank You for Not Being There!"

The 2007 SEA Games in December was hosted in the northern Thai city of Nakhon Ratchasima for the first time, in conjunction with the 80th birthday of the long-serving monarch King Bhumibol Adulyadej.

Of the 24 athletes sent in by the Singapore Athletics Association, there was one glaring omission. For the first time since 1987, James Wong would not feature in Team Singapore's roster at the Games. The thrower had made good on his declaration to call time on his career.

While this was a massive loss for Singapore, it also represented a chance for someone else to profit.

After 12 years of playing second fiddle, Wansawang Sawasdee finally struck gold in the discus. He was an outstanding thrower who was just unlucky enough to reach his competitive peak at the same time as the mercurial James Wong. In front of an adoring home crowd at the His Majesty the King's 80th Birthday Sports Complex, he finally added a gold to his overflowing chest of silver medals.

James recalled a light-hearted conversation he had with Wansawang after that moment.

"He was so happy with the win and would always tell me how grateful he was to me that I didn't show up in 2007. 'Thank you for not being there!' he would say to me."

Despite their rivalry in the discus ring, both men had actually forged a respectful friendship through the heat of numerous battles that raged across different Southeast Asian cities over the past 12 years.

Reflecting on 2007, the only SEA Games edition he missed in a sports career spanning a quarter of a century, James maintains that he has no regrets.

"Many people point to this moment as a blemish on my record, a broken link in my gold medal streak. At that point in 2006–2007, I just felt that the sporting ecosystem wasn't conducive enough for me to train at my best. Even if I wanted to continue, there were no guarantees that under such a system, I could even produce my best to continue winning. I was ready to fight on, but without the support, it just all felt pointless to me. I decided then that it was the right time to step away and have never regretted this decision."

PART SIX Setbacks...

Although both men were fierce rivals in the discus ring, James and Wansawang were good friends outside of the arena. Below, Wansawang is pictured with young Jessica and Jordan.

· Part Seven ·

... and Comebacks

Chapter 29

The Last Push

17 July 2023

James made a long-awaited visit to see his oncologist once more concerning the resumption of his chemotherapy treatment. Since his second surgery, he was anxious to return to his cancer treatment again.

Since his discharge, he had returned to the hospital to not only remove his stitches, but also to perform another battery of tests just to make sure that the intestinal issues would not surface again. The doctors also took the liberty to check his heart health via an ECG test to ensure that he did not experience atrial fibrillation like what happened after his first surgery. No stone was left unturned to make sure he was in the best shape to resume his treatment.

He was also advised to make some dietary changes. He was told to eat less fibrous foods as well as to chew his food to smaller pieces before swallowing. This was meant to prevent his intestines from overworking and, as a result, twisting again.

PART SEVEN  ... and Comebacks

At the time of his second surgery, he had only managed to complete four of his eight chemotherapy cycles. After checking his blood markers, he was told by his oncologist that he could now start with his fifth cycle and pick up where he left off.

His blood markers continued to show promising signs that his recovery was on track. This prompted the oncologist to suggest that he upped the dosage from five Xeloda pills per morning/evening cycle to six. This increment would begin gradually from the start of the fifth cycle all the way to the eighth and final cycle.

Although nervous about the side effects, the athlete in James was also anxious to see positive results. Hence, he readily agreed.

"I could not believe the difference one extra pill made in terms of side effects. The frequency of tummy aches and bloatedness started to increase. There was increased soreness in my fingers and the skin along my finger joints started to peel and split. This made simple tasks like carrying plastic bags or even removing bottle caps difficult."

Drawing from his sports experiences, he said, "This final stretch felt like the last push towards the SEA Games. It was either I go hard or go home. I told myself to push on, knowing that my recovery was on the line. Making comebacks was after all nothing new to me."

Chapter 30

"8possible"

February 2009

Under usual circumstances, seeing a 40-year-old participant line up in an athletics event would not create so much as a stir or any other major reaction. However, at the Second All-Comers Meet organised at Bukit Gombak Stadium, all eyes were transfixed on a particular middle-aged veteran at the discus cage competing alongside athletes who were almost half his age. He was clearly dominating the competition as he flung discus after discus onto the field, leaving his competitors in a mix of awe and embarrassment for failing to keep up. Although his final result was a subdued 47-metre distance, the message he sent out was resoundingly clear: James Wong is back!

"Motivation is very important for me. I need a reason to carry on. There were several that made me decide on this comeback. Firstly, Team Singapore only captured one athletics gold medal in 2007 and

PART SEVEN ... and Comebacks

it saddened me that we had not improved. I felt that even at my age, I could still come back and do something for the sport. The second reason was a more personal one. The 2009 SEA Games would be held in Laos for the first time, and I wanted to be able to compete and win at every nation that the SEA Games was ever hosted in. That would be a personal achievement for me. Moreover, which athlete can lay claim to having competed at every ASEAN nation that hosted the SEA Games before?"

While his run-ins with the Singapore Athletics Association (SAA) over the past few years were highly publicised, James made it a point this time to avoid controversy by limiting contact and making necessary financial arrangements to wean himself off any dependence on the association. He had just started a new job as a lecturer at the Nanyang Polytechnic's (NYP's) Sports and Wellness Department in 2007. The polytechnic had a well-known reputation for its strong and unwavering support of athletics. Thus, he had all the facilities at his disposal to train once more.

He summed up his position succinctly: "All I needed from the SAA was to nominate me for the Games if I met the qualifying mark, and to send me if I qualified for any competitions on my own merit."

The publicity surrounding his comeback was quickly ramped up into overdrive. On his own initiative, James pitched a marketing idea to his sponsor Adidas to use the tagline "8possible" to mark his comeback. This was a clever play on his personal hunt for his eighth discus gold, as well as on Adidas' own marketing slogan, "Impossible is Nothing". Adidas gifted him a pair of custom shoes with "8possible" printed on them.

Right around the time of James' announcement, the SAA was experiencing some troubles of its own. To many observers, Loh Lin Kok's election victory in 2008 did not deliver the necessary changes that were promised. A number of issues were brought to the fore which seriously dented the SAA's credibility to run the sport. These included the seemingly lack of transparency in selection criteria and the shocking revelation that the SAA had been late to submit their high-performance plans for the next financial year, causing the Singapore Sports Council to withhold funding until the plans had been sorted out.

This, together with a lack of progress at international meets, culminated in a petition signed by more than 100 athletes, coaches, administrators, and parents calling for a vote of no-confidence in President Loh's team.

In the lead-up to the SEA Games, veteran sports administrators and even politicians like the then Minister for Community Development, Youth and Sports Vivian Balakrishnan, along with then Deputy Prime Minister and President of the Singapore National Olympic Council Teo Chee Hean, joined in the chorus calling for the SAA to sort out the mess and step up their game.

PART SEVEN ... and Comebacks

It was under these storm clouds that James arrived in Vientiane, the capital city of Laos to reclaim his discus title in December 2009, and perhaps bring some much-needed cheer to Singapore athletics.

Far from being distracted by the controversy, he felt vindicated by his decision to return.

"If anything, all the negative reports in the media about athletics clearly justified my reason to return. The sport is very close to my heart, I could not let it die out like this. I may be 40 at the time, but I think I still have plenty to offer to Singapore athletics. I wouldn't be here if I didn't think I could win."

The veteran thrower shook off the dust accumulated from his hiatus since his last SEA Games outing in 2005 and took the lead with his first throw at 52.18 metres. His two Thai rivals Kvanchai Numsomboon and Wansawang Sawasdee both kept up the pace with 52.15 and 52.02 metres, respectively.

The pressure was ramped up when James fouled out on his second and third attempts. His fourth gave him some respite when he stretched the lead to 52.53 metres, but it was still a slender margin.

"8possible"

Winding into a discus rotation. James was determined to recapture his discus crown in Vientiane in 2009 which he relinquished back in 2007 by virtue of not competing.

PART SEVEN  ... and Comebacks

He watched on nervously as the two Thais continued to dog his heels in search of the breakthrough, to keep the hard-won discus title from 2007 in Thai hands. Ultimately, it proved a bridge too far for them. After their sixth attempt in which they failed to match James' leading distance, the big man stood up in victory.

However, he was not done. He strode up to the discus cage, signalling to officials that he would take his final throw despite having already won. There he spun and hurled the discus to a new season's best of 53.60 metres.

When asked why he bothered to take his final attempt, he gave a cheekily audacious response that was typical of him. "I didn't want them going home thinking James Wong beat them only by a few centimetres!"

Chapter 31

The Other Side of the Fence

Although his victory was meant to give some breathing room to the beleaguered Singapore Athletics Association (SAA), it ended up having the opposite effect as it intensified the criticism of the association — that it had to rely on a 40-year-old man who existed outside of their high-performance orbit to continue bringing home the gold medals.

The victory also stirred up a political awakening in James, who started to feel that he could use his experience and standing in the sport as a means to deliver real change. He first reached out to athletics legend C. Kunalan to discuss ideas and changes that the sport needed. The resultant meeting proved to be a fruitful one. However, both men realised that they needed a public figure with sufficient standing to unite the fraternity.

In early 2010, the two athletics luminaries paid a visit to the Bukit Timah home of Tang Weng Fei, the former president of the SAA from

PART SEVEN ... and Comebacks

James with former SAA president Tang Weng Fei. Both men forged a successful partnership that helped shaped the future of the post-Loh Lin Kok era of athletics.

2004 to 2006. Tang was initially groomed to be Loh Lin Kok's successor, but eventually stepped down in frustration after his solitary term following a series of high-profile disputes concerning athletes and coaches in 2005 and 2006. James recalled that Tang had always been a voice of reason amidst all his disputes with the SAA back then and still retained strong ground support from many coaches, athletes, and officials due to his generosity and affable personality. It did not take long for Tang to be won over by their pitch.

A solid team consisting of former national athletes, coaches, and sports administrators was quickly assembled to contest the 2010 elections against the incumbent Loh. James would serve as honorary secretary to this team.

Facing pressure from all sides, Loh took the unprecedented move to announce his shock withdrawal from the presidential race, leaving the door wide open for Tang to make his return to the hot seat as president of the SAA.

James' profile as a sports administrator was also boosted by another significant appointment in 2010. That year, Singapore made sporting history by becoming the host of the inaugural Youth Olympic Games (YOG). The Singapore National Olympic Council (SNOC) announced that James would have the honour of serving as chef de mission of the Singapore contingent at the Games.

In a ringing endorsement of his qualities, SNOC's secretary-general Chris Chan told the media that "James is a very good role model and also active with our athletes. He also has experience as an athlete at major games. [...] He is vocal and will speak up for the athletes."

His experience at the YOG would quickly orient him to the challenges and tasks that he would face in his years ahead as a sports administrator.

"The role was an honour, but I also understood the magnitude of the tasks ahead of me. There were so many sports we had to oversee, all with their unique requests and considerations. You need a lot of patience and a big heart to help athletes in this job. As much as I tried to help, resources were also finite. If I couldn't help, I at least tried to listen. Being on the other side of the fence as an administrator really opened my eyes to the challenges that these officials so often face behind the scenes in preparing Team Singapore for major games."

Chapter 32

"The Flag Bearer Must Win the Gold."

In February 2011, James announced once more that he would return to defend his discus title at the SEA Games in Palembang, Indonesia. He would be gunning for his ninth discus gold, and 10th overall gold medal at the Games.

He revisited the issue of motivation again.

"Since the SAA management team was new, we needed some solid results to raise the profile of the team. As a member of the committee, I wanted to do my part."

But it was apparent that his title defence would not be that easy this time round.

"I was trying to juggle my training, my job at NYP as well as my committee work with the SAA. On top of that, I had started coaching as well, and was working with a talented young female thrower [Wan] Lay Chi, who was also a *medal contender at the Games. I remembered starting my day with training at six in the morning, before turning in close to midnight, after I had finished all my tasks.*

"Training-wise, age was definitely catching up. While I used to put in 40 quality throws per training session, I could only manage an average of 25 now. I could feel aches and pains the next morning whenever I trained.

"While regional standards in the discus had not improved significantly, my performances were regressing to the point that my rivals were within touching distance of me. The Thais would always be contenders, and Indonesia was also backing an up-and-coming thrower to challenge me.

"I knew I had my work cut out for me this time."

All these factors finally came to a breaking point for James, who decided to quit his Nanyang Polytechnic (NYP) job and join the Singapore Athletics Association (SAA) full-time as its sports performance manager in June 2011. This move provided him with a much-needed respite to declutter his hectic life. In order to take on his managerial role as a member of the SAA Secretariat, he had to relinquish his committee position as honorary secretary. In a sense, the SAA role became his full-time job. It was a move that suited him well given his love for the sport.

To help keep his focus on the SEA Games, he enlisted the help of a former colleague at NYP to decorate his throwing shoes with all

PART SEVEN ... and Comebacks

Shoes fit for a king. The decorated pair of shoes which James wore for the 2011 SEA Games. A painted reminder of his unrelenting determination to win.

the gold medals he had accumulated so far from the Games. Right at the centre of the shoe in front of the laces was the centrepiece — a blank circular slot to remind him of the gold medal he needed to win.

To heap more pressure on his hefty shoulders, he was once again selected by the Singapore National Olympic Council (SNOC) to lift the national flag at the Palembang Games, serving as the Singapore contingent's flag bearer.

While this was a great honour for him, even though it was his second time, the appointment came with a price.

"To my dismay, the organisers scheduled the discus as the first event on the morning after the opening ceremony. I knew the ceremony would involve a lot of waiting and standing, and would probably go on till late in the evening. But letting my country down was not an option. There were people who fought for me to take up

"The Flag Bearer Must Win the Gold."

Flag bearer once more. James received the national flag from the late Dr. Tan Eng Liang who was serving as chef de mission of the Singapore contingent at the 2011 Palembang SEA Games.

PART SEVEN ... and Comebacks

James started off the 2011 SEA Games discus competition sluggishly, before momentum swung in his favour.

this honoured role. If I had to stand the whole night and try to compete the next day just to repay their faith, I would do it. I'm traditional in that sense. To me, the flag bearer has to win the gold medal. I wanted to do it for Singapore no matter how challenging it was."

"The Flag Bearer Must Win the Gold."

The long hours spent at the opening ceremony likely caused James to start off sluggishly. After his first three attempts, he had not only fouled twice, but failed to crack 50 metres. After yet another infringement for stepping outside of the ring during his third attempt, he roared in frustration as the nervous Singapore camp watched on. He was trailing in second behind the Thai thrower Kvanchai Numsomboon, who had recorded 50.28 metres.

"Enough games!" he chided himself, slapping his face and thighs.

Then, he clicked into a different gear. Releasing the discus to a blood-curdling battle cry, he knew that he had found his sweet spot again the moment it left his hands. He was celebrating with another resounding cry even before the distance was measured, to general applause from the stands.

The scoreboard only confirmed what he already knew. He had taken the lead with 51.32 metres on his fourth attempt. With his engine now whirring and chugging away, momentum was irreversibly swung in his favour as he posted two more impressive attempts over 50 metres, confirming his victory once more.

Holding the national flag aloft, he paraded in front of the Singapore camp to acknowledge his supporters, who counted Deputy Prime Minister Teo Chee Hean among them. The President of the SNOC had woken up bright and early in time to witness James Wong win Singapore's first gold medal at the 2011 SEA Games.

For the 10th time in his storied SEA Games career, he stood on the podium listening to *Majulah Singapura* echo around the stadium.

PART SEVEN ... and Comebacks

Almost 43 years of age at this point, James showed no signs of slowing down and he powered through to achieve another gold medal in the discus. The three Singaporeans standing directly in front of him are Teo Chee Hean (Deputy Prime Minister, left), Maurice Nicholas (General Secretary of the Asian Athletics Association, centre), and Tang Weng Fei (President of Singapore Athletics Association, right).

It was a moment that was so significant for him, and one that he never grew tired of.

Once again, he paid tribute to Jana for his victory.

"I often wish I had been able to spend more time with her and my family. If she wasn't an athlete herself, she wouldn't have understood why I was doing this. Her support meant everything to me."

"The Flag Bearer Must Win the Gold."

In what was fast becoming an amusing ritual, he declared his retirement for the umpteenth time to spend more time with his family. However, his wife knew better.

"Oh I don't think we've seen the last of James Wong," she gave a knowing grin while speaking to *The New Paper* after the competition.

Jana served as both coach and cheerleader to her husband in 2011 as they celebrated another victory together.

· Part Eight ·

The Last Gold

PART EIGHT The Last Gold

Chapter 33

History Beckons

February 2013

When James announced that he would try for the 2013 SEA Games held at Nay Pyi Taw, Myanmar's newly designated capital city, it drew mixed reactions this time rather than the general sense of relief that usually accompanied these announcements.

Journalists and sports administrators alike started to question the impact of the 44-year-old veteran's latest comeback.

Writing for *The New Paper*, journalist Leonard Thomas lamented how this move could hamper the development of new talents in the context of Singapore relying on veteran sports athletes and administrators. "Experience makes for cool heads and correct decision-making under fire [...] But in a thriving ecosystem, there should be a production line of talent humming nicely [...] That does not seem to be the case right now."

PART EIGHT  The Last Gold

These sentiments were also shared by Singapore National Olympic Council (SNOC) Secretary-General Chris Chan who told *The Straits Times* that "it's disappointing in a way because I hope we don't have to keep depending on James to deliver the results for Singapore".

James was nevertheless unfazed.

"I knew what people were saying. But I was clear about my reasons. I could still contribute to Team Singapore. Besides, I have not been to Myanmar for the SEA Games, and a gold medal there will make another fine addition to my collection."

Indeed, the last time Myanmar hosted the Games in 1969 just happened to be the year James was born.

Being a devotee of statistics, he combed through the Singapore Athletics Association's archives and discovered that he was on the cusp of making unique history at the SEA Games.

In the Games' athletics history, the most gold medals won by the same athlete in a single event was nine. This distinction was held by Myanmar thrower Jennifer Tin Lay, who blitzed a total of nine shot put and six discus gold medals across a shimmering 28-year career at the SEA Games starting from the 1967 SEAP Games held in Bangkok. Incidentally, she bowed out after the 1985 Games, just one edition before James made his competitive debut in 1987.

Once James was made aware of this record, he was consumed with a single-minded focus to push on and to become the most bemedalled athlete in a single athletics event in the Games' history. Both throwers were now tied at nine apiece. Winning the gold medal

Two titans of SEA Games athletics. James Wong and the legendary Jennifer Tin Lay of Myanmar, who was serving as an official at the 2013 SEA Games hosted in her home country. Together, both athletes amassed a staggering total of 35 SEA Games medals spanning 1967 to 2013.

at Nay Pyi Taw would break the deadlock in James' favour. It felt like destiny was calling him to break the record in Myanmar, where his co-record holder was from.

However, age was not on his side. For the first time in his career, trying to meet the previous edition's bronze medal qualifying mark would not come easy. After numerous attempts, he finally came the closest at the Taiwan Open in May where he threw his season's best of 50.06 metres, though he was still 22 centimetres from the qualifying.

On account of his proximity to the qualifying mark as well as his unparalleled track record of producing big performances when it

PART EIGHT The Last Gold

Almost 45 years of age and no longer the athlete he once was, James fought to the very end against competitors half his age, achieving a season's best.

mattered at the Games, the SNOC gave him the final nod to compete. He would repay the faith by heaving to 50.59 metres in November at the Malaysian Open, just one month before the games. Still, this only ranked him fourth in terms of season's best among the competitors. This was a clear and unmistakable sign that he was no longer the dominant force at the SEA Games.

As part of his preparations, James studied the recent performances of his closest rivals. He had identified the Thais Kvanchai Numsomboon and Narong Benjaroon, as well as the Indonesian Hermanto as potential threats. However, a new up-and-coming 18-year-old Malaysian would escape his notice.

Although he knew who Muhammad Irfan Shamsuddin was and they had competed together on some occasions that year, the younger thrower had never thrown beyond 50 metres. James did not see him as a threat.

Yet at the Wunna Theikdi Stadium at Nay Pyi Taw, the young contender announced his arrival on his final throw where he spun and heaved his discus across the newly-laid field to snatch the gold medal with 53.16 metres. After 20 long years since 1993, James Wong had been beaten at a SEA Games discus competition. He ended up with a season's best at 50.82 metres, finishing in fifth, his worst ever showing at the SEA Games.

Upon seeing the digits on the electronic scoreboard, the young Malaysian sprinted to the field, prostrated himself on the grass and kissed the green turf. It was an emotional moment for the young kingslayer who would establish himself as a force of nature in the discus event in his own right.

James, demonstrating magnanimity in defeat, walked up to the new champion to shake his hand.

PART EIGHT The Last Gold

James demonstrates magnanimity in defeat by shaking the hand of Muhammad Irfan Shamsuddin of Malaysia who had dethroned him as the king of Southeast Asian discus.

"Break my record if you can," he challenged the Malaysian while their hands were still locked in a firm handshake.

The new champion quickly paid tribute in a post-competition interview to the veteran he dethroned. "Since I was 16, I've been hearing the name 'James Wong'. Sometimes, I wonder how he can keep doing it because of his age. So you have to give him some respect."

James was philosophical about his defeat. "I had produced my season's best against a very strong field. In any other edition of the Games, anything above 50 metres would guarantee you a medal. But not this time. I'm happy that a worthy successor has taken my place and that the standard of Southeast Asian discus is finally improving. Of course I wanted the gold, but this was not a bad way to go out as well."

In 1995 right after his discus victory in Chiang Mai, James spoke about about his sporting retirement, telling the media that ending his career when Singapore next hosted the Games would be special for him. Initially, the republic was supposed to have hosted the Games some time in the middle to late 2000s. However, delays in the demolition and construction of the National Stadium pushed this timeline further back until it was eventually fixed at 2015, on the 50th year of the nation's independence.

When he was asked if he would return as promised in 2015 when Singapore would once again host the SEA Games for the first time since 1993, there was a greater air of finality about his response this time.

"Not a chance! Time for me to kick back and watch the young ones throw," he said with some sense of relief.

This time, the public believed him.

Chapter 34

The Survivor

October 2023

Completing his eight cycles of chemotherapy felt like a graduation of sorts for James.

"I was just so glad to have completed it. The side effects were in full force for the last couple of weeks. There was the usual soreness and aches, as well tenderness in my fingers. The hardest one to get over was the fact that my taste buds were affected. I have enjoyed cooking from the years I spent overseas, and it became tough for me to do so because I couldn't taste the food. I had to rely on my experience and gut feeling to get the dishes right."

When he finally received his blood test results after his final cycle, everything seemed normal. For decades, he had tested his limits and boundaries to achieve extraordinary feats. Now, he had never been more happy to be "ordinary" again.

Or, as he so animatedly described it, "It's like opening a Christmas present to know that I was in the clear for now."

Jana recalled the relief she felt at the moment.

"The family was happy for sure. But there was always that nagging feeling that it could come back. But I know James. He's a survivor. He has faced numerous battles in life and this was no different. We knew he could handle it."

The battle was far from won, however. The possibility of a relapse was always there, and he needed to submit himself to regular testing over the next five years to be sure. The testing interval would be months apart at first, progressing to a year or two if there were no abnormalities in his results.

But for now, he could move on with his life away from hospitals, doctors, surgeries, and blood tests. Yet some aspects of his life would be irreversibly altered.

"I have always been a lover of food. It will be challenging to maintain my weight at 105–110 kilograms. I also can't take alcohol like I used to, since I only have half my pancreas left. But all things considered, I am happy to get most of my life back, to be able to enjoy simple delights like spending time with my family and loved ones."

Enduring a cancer ordeal also transformed James into an impassioned advocate for cancer awareness, good lifestyle habit, and early detection.

> *"This second chance in life has made me reflective of how my journey can serve as a guide to others who are treading this same difficult path. Maintaining a balanced and healthy lifestyle does go a long way to support wellness*

PART EIGHT  The Last Gold

and quality of life. This includes eating in moderation and ensuring a balanced diet.

"By instilling a habit of attending regular medical checkups, one can identify and address any underlying health issues promptly, ensuring that necessary treatment can be rendered in a timely fashion. On top of this, it is also important to stay attuned to your body's warning signals. Any sudden appearance of signs or symptoms can sometimes highlight emerging health concerns. Do not be afraid to seek medical advice in such situations. This can often make the difference between life and death.

"Regular exercise does play a part in promoting cardiovascular health, strengthening the heart and improving blood circulation to our vital organs. These are vital defence mechanisms that can strengthen your immunity against disease.

"The vital thread weaving all these aspects together is consistency. These holistic health habits require a sustained commitment towards prioritising your health through various stages of life. My ordeal has certainly made me more aware and appreciative of the habits I could and should have adopted. I hope others can find this advice enlightening."

The entire experience also changed the lives and perspectives of his family.

Jessica had relocated back to Singapore permanently to be closer to her family. "My father had been through so much this past year with so many scares in between. I wasn't around for all of them. I just didn't want to be away again should something untoward happen."

Jordan also cited how his father's fighting spirit had inspired him. "My father has always been an inspiration to my sporting journey. This past year, I saw him in a different light. I saw how he walked the talk by taking on his personal challenges head-on without complaints or fuss. It dawned on me why he became the athlete that he was. I am definitely inspired to work harder in my own sporting journey."

Chapter 35

A Final Word
by James Wong

I don't usually regret my decisions in life. I believe everything good or bad happens for a reason.

I still remember very vividly, that first bus journey from school to the Kallang Practice Track. So much doubt and uncertainty were racing through my mind as the bus ambled slowly along Pasir Panjang Road to Keppel and Nicoll Highway. I was stepping into the unknown based on a hunch, a gut feeling to seek out a simple purpose in life, a sense of direction for my youthful restlessness. I didn't know what awaited me at the track, whether the coaches would take me in or even accept a young upstart like me, walking into their training session with such brazen audacity. Athletes were scouted and invited to be part of these sessions. I simply showed up and knocked on the door, armed with only a school sports day medal and poor technique as my resume.

That moment changed my life forever. It opened doors that an average kampung boy like me could never have dreamed of. That I could represent my nation and compete in exotic locations around the world, that I could get a university degree in America or meet my lovely wife and life partner in Germany. If you told that 14-year-old boy that all these would happen just by getting on that bus, he would never have believed you.

I also remember that moment when cancer revealed its ghastly face to me. It was like time stood still. Every single detail in the doctor's office is carved into my memory: the time on his room clock, the placement of stationery on his desk, the layout of his room. My first reaction was typical of all cancer patients: "Why me, why now?" My life had been going well, my children were grown up and beginning to find their place in the world. My wife and I were looking forward to and planning for our retirement.

Suddenly, I had to worry about things that I usually never gave a second thought to. I was contacting lawyers to prepare a will, I was getting in touch with my financial planners to check my insurance coverage. I felt ill-equipped and inadequate to deal with what life had thrown at me, just as I would feel uncomfortable going into competitions unprepared.

Then I came to the bitter realisation that the disease does not discriminate. You could be a blue-collar worker, a CEO, or a 10-time SEA Games gold medallist, it did not matter. There is no hiding from this deadly lottery of misery and death.

After recovering from the initial shock, I am glad my athlete conditioning instinctively took over. I recalled the careful and meticulous

PART EIGHT The Last Gold

A collection of every single medal James had amassed from the SEA Games from a storied career lasting 1987 to 2013.

Winner's mascots. James' SEA Games adventures are also told through the Games' mascots he had collected over the years, each bearing the traditions and symbolism of their host country.

A Final Word

preparations I had put in ahead of each of those SEA Games campaigns and resolved to enact the same battle plan in my fight against the disease. I stuck to a carefully prepared exercise and diet regimen in my pre-surgery prep, as well as my post-surgery recovery. I have faced impossible odds before. I've been written off, been told at different junctures that I was too young, too cocky, or too old to win. More often than not, I have proven my detractors wrong. This fight would be no different.

To succeed in sports, athletes need to have a certain amount of eccentricity. This could manifest itself in different ways like arrogance, competitiveness, or stubbornness. It takes a certain amount of craziness to keep doing what we do, sacrificing so much of our personal lives in the process. Many only see the medals and podium finishes, but not the hard work we put in behind the scenes to get there. I would need every ounce of this "craziness" to keep going on the difficult path laid out before me.

If there's one thing the experience with cancer taught me, is that family will always be the most important thing. Just as my wife stood by me all those years while I was competing, she never left my side throughout those difficult moments at the hospital or at the doctor's office. My children also showed how much they had grown and matured when they stepped forward to care for me. I'm proud of the confident young adults that they have grown up to be. I'm also grateful to all the friends and relatives who have shown care and concern through it all.

This battle will not be won easily nor quickly. Even with my chemotherapy cycles concluded, a relapse will always be a possibility,

PART EIGHT: The Last Gold

A Final Word

no matter how slim. Similar to an Olympic cycle of four years, I'm prepared to fight on for the long haul. My eye is on the final prize: complete recovery. In between, I have to make sure my lifestyle habits continue to support my recovery. Even if cancer should rear its ugly head again to me, I want it to be known that I'll be fighting every step of the way. As I like to remind my rivals in the discus ring, it's not over until James Wong has finished all his six throws.

This struggle will bear the highest stakes among all my battles. When you fail in sports, you can always get up and try again. But when you lose to a terminal disease, you don't get a second chance. When I stepped into the Kallang field all those years ago as a 14-year-old boy to start my athletics journey, I wasn't just trying to win glory for my country and myself, I was actually preparing for this moment 40 years later. I just didn't know it then.

Like all my other SEA Games wins, I believe I shall emerge victorious from this setback. This battle I faced over the past year will stand head and shoulders above all my other victories.

This triumph will be worthy of my last dance in life — my last gold.

James Wong's Career Highlights

Date	Event
10 January 1969	James Wong was born. He is the fifth of six children in his family.
June–August 1984	Joined the SSC A&W Athletic Programme that was headed by visiting American coach Gary Stenlund at the Kallang Practice Track. Stenlund departed in Aug 1984, leaving James in the care of local coach Fok Keng Choy.
10 November 1984	Broke the U17 and U15 national records in the discus with 38.90m (1.5kg)[8] at the 5th All Comers Meet.
19 May 1985	Broke the U17 national record in the discus with 42.30m (1.5kg) at the 1st All Comers Meet.
9 July 1985	Broke the National Schools Track and Field Championship B Division and national U19 discus record with 45.20m (1.5kg).
10 April 1986	Broke the national record in the discus with 41.56m at the Thailand Open.
28 June 1986	Broke the U19 discus national record with 46.90m (1.5kg) at the Flash Sports Club Annual Track and Field Meet.
10 July 1986	Broke the National Schools Track and Field Championship B Division and national U19 Discus record with 47.40m (1.5kg).
10 August 1986	Broke the ASEAN Schools Athletics Championships and national U19 record with 47.42m (1.5kg).
8 November 1986	Became first Southeast Asian junior athlete to surpass 50m in the discus with 52.22m effort (1.5kg), also breaking the national U19 record.

---

[8] All discus weight implements are set at 2kg unless otherwise stated.

4 February 1987	Broke the national record in the discus with 44.52m at Thai Inter-Club Track and Field Championships.
15 February 1987	Broke the national record with 46.30m at the 1st All Comers Meet.
28 April 1987	Set the Philippines Open championship and Philippines All-Comers record with 45.37m.
26 May 1987	Broke the national record with 46.68m at the Hong Kong-Singapore Inter-Port Series.
14 June 1987	Broke the national record with 47.98m at the Federal Territory Open. This result also surpassed the SEA Games record of 47.78m. This was James' fifth national record of the year.
29 July 1987	Broke the National Schools Track and Field Championships A Division record with 52.00m (1.5kg).
17 September 1987	**14th SEA Games (Jakarta)** Made SEA Games debut, finishing in third in the discus with 44.86m.
25 August 1989	**15th SEA Games (Kuala Lumpur)** Clinched silver in the discus with 47.96m, missing the gold medal by 8cm.
September 1990	Enrolled in Mt. San Antonio College to pursue a pre-university diploma and train. He took up the hammer event in America as well.
September 1991	Made his World Athletics Championships debut in Tokyo, throwing 44.26m and failing to qualify for the next round.
December 1991	**16th SEA Games (Manila)** Finished in fourth for both the hammer (48.00m) and discus (47.68m). This would be the first time he returned from the Games without a medal.
March 1992	Broke the national Hammer record with 52.42m at a meet in Arizona.

August 1992	Enrolled in Angelo State University to pursue a degree in Kinesiology.
March 1993	Broke the national discus record twice, first with 49.70m, then with 50.24m, going beyond 50m for the first time with the 2kg implement. Also broke the national shot put record with 14.12m.
April 1993	Broke both discus (51.02m) and hammer (55.40m) national records.
June 1993	**17th SEA Games (Singapore)** Won Singapore's first Athletics gold medal at the SEA Games since 1983 with 49.02m in the discus. Also won a silver in the hammer with 52.86m.
1 April 1995	Broke shot put (15.03m) and hammer (56.13m) national records in Texas.
6 May 1995	Broke national discus record with 50.74m at the University of Texas Arlington Meet.
14 May 1995	Broke national discus record with 51.66m at the Abilene Christian University All Comers Meet.
27 May 1995	Broke national hammer record with 56.36m at the NCAA Division 2 Championships, finishing in third.
May 1995	Graduated from Angelo State University.
3 June 1995	Embarked on a training stint in Halle, Germany
20 August 1995	Broke the national discus record with 52.98m at a meet in Norden, Germany less than three months into his training stint.
December 1995	**18th SEA Games (Chiangmai)** Successfully defended the discus title with 49.88m. Broke national record in the hammer with 56.68m, but finished second.

James Wong's Career Highlights

July 1996	Denied participation in the Atlanta Olympics as the nation was only allowed to send one male athlete in the absence of any athlete who qualified for the Olympics. The Singapore Amateur Athletics Association (SAAA) opted to send high jumper Wong Yew Tong.
27 September 1997	Broke national discus record with 54.08m at the Singapore Open.
October 1997	**19th SEA Games (Jakarta)** Won the double gold in the discus (52.18m) and hammer (58.00m) events, setting a new national record in the hammer, and a new SEA Games record in the discus.
September–November 1998	Missed the Commonwealth and Asian Games due to a wrist injury.
7 April 1999	Broke national hammer record with 58.20m in Halle.
8 May 1999	Broke national discus record with 59.87m in Wiesbaden, Germany.
August 1999	**20th SEA Games (Bandar Seri Begawan)** Won gold in the discus setting a new SEA Games record with 59.50m. The record is still standing at the time of this book's writing in 2024. Finished second in the hammer event and declared his intention to quit the hammer. SAAA President Loh Lin Kok branded him a failure for this loss.
March–April 2000	Declared intention to quit athletics after the SAAA failed to nominate him for the Singapore National Olympic Council Sports Awards. Involved in a highly publicised spat with SAAA officials in the media.

13 April 2000	Received a Meritorious Award at the SNOC Sports Awards after the SAAA performed a u-turn and nominated James. He reaffirmed his decision to quit full-time training to start a new career as a strength and conditioning coach with the newly set up Sports Medicine and Sports Science Division in the SSC.
June 2001	Announced his intention to compete at the SEA Games that year.
August 2001	**21st SEA Games (Kuala Lumpur)** Won gold in the discus with 56.98m. In total, he spent 24 hours in Kuala Lumpur before returning to Singapore.
December 2003	**22nd SEA Games (Hanoi)** Won gold in the discus with 56.49m. He was the Singapore contingent's flag bearer at the Games.
20 April 2004	Won Sportsman of the Year at the SNOC Sports Awards.
July 2004	Awarded the Singapore Youth Award in the Sports and Entrepreneurship category for his contribution to sport. Also selected to represent Singapore as a torch bearer in the Olympic Torch Relay leading up to the Athens Olympics.
August 2005	Struck by dengue right before the 23rd SEA Games in November. He is bedridden for days and unable to train. Had to restart his training preparation from an almost zero state with only three months to go to the SEA Games.
November 2005	**23rd SEA Games (Manila)** Won gold in the discus with 55.11m in his weakened state, fending off a determined challenge by Thai rival Wansawang Sawasdee. Also won bronze in the shot put event.

April–May 2006	Embarked on a training trip to Thailand and Germany in an attempt to qualify for the Asian Games in Doha.
September 2006	Failed to meet the Asian Games qualifying distance of 57.78m with his closest attempt being 56.06m. The Singapore Athletics Association (SAA) declined to appeal for him and he was not selected for the Games. Announced his intention to quit due to lack of support from the SAA.
December 2007	**24th SEA Games (Korat)** The first time since 1987 where James did not take part in the SEA Games. In his absence, the discus title was won by his close competitor, Wansawang Sawasdee.
February 2009	Announced his intention to compete at the SEA Games that year, citing his "disappointment" with Team Singapore's athletics results at the 2007 SEA Games as a reason for his comeback.
May 2009	Appointed Chef de Mission for the Singapore contingent at the inaugural Youth Olympics Games in 2010.
December 2009	**25th SEA Games (Vientiane)** Won gold at the discus event with 53.60m.
May 2009	Joined former SAA President Tang Weng Fei's team as Honorary Secretary to contest the SAA elections. Following incumbent Loh Lin Kok's retirement, Tang's team which included James was swept into office.
April 2011	Quit his Honorary Secretary post to join SAA as General Manager, a full-time secretariat position. Announced his intention to compete at the 2011 SEA Games to support the new management team.

November 2011	**26th SEA Games (Palembang)** Won gold at the discus event with 51.32m. This was the 10th gold medal in his SEA Games career.
December 2013	**27th SEA Games (Nay Pyi Taw)** Finished fifth in the discus with 50.82m. This is the first time in SEA Games history that a throw above 50m was not enough for a medal. This was also the second time in James' SEA Games career that he would return home without a medal. He announced his sporting retirement for the final time just one month shy of his 45th birthday.

James Wong's Cancer Timeline (2023)

Date	Event
20 January 2023	After experiencing yellowing of his skin and eyes, James went to Changi General Hospital (CGH) for medical advice. He was diagnosed with Obstructive Jaundice after initial blood tests indicated high levels of bilirubin in his system. He was warded for further tests.
25 January	A CT scan detected a 2cm growth obstructing his bile duct, confirming the reason why his bilirubin levels were high.
26 January	An oral scope and biopsy confirmed that the obstruction was in fact a cancerous tumour. James was thus diagnosed as having Stage 2 Bile Duct Cancer (Distal Bile Duct Cholangiocarcinoma). The hospital recommended Whipple surgery to remove the tumour. A plastic stent was also inserted in his bile duct to bypass the blockage of the tumour to relieve the jaundice.
30 January	Discharged from CGH and began planning his pre-surgery fitness routine with support from his family. Was reviewed by the anaesthetic team and prehabilitation team for preparation of operation.
24 February	Day of the Whipple procedure. Due to careful dieting and a vigorous exercise regime, James managed to reduce his weight from 126 to 121kg in three weeks, improving on his upper and lower body strength as well. The surgery took about 11 hours and was declared a success. Post operatively, he was transferred to the high dependency ward to recover.

28 February	After attempting to stretch his legs, James' heart rate skyrocketed to 215 beats per minute. After medication, his heart rate was lowered to 160 in the evening.
1 March	The medical team confirmed that he had suffered from atrial fibrillation which caused his heart rate to spike. After further medication, his heart rate was brought back to normal levels.
3 March	Transferred to a normal ward. By this point, he was able to consume solid food and move short distances with some assistance.
5 March	Discharged well from CGH for recovery at home nine days after operation. After discharge, James had to adjust to new dietary and exercise routines. He had to eat in moderation as well as to resume his walks to support his recovery process.
27 March	Visited the oncologist to discuss his chemotherapy treatment.
17 April	Began chemotherapy treatment. This consisted of consuming five xeloda pills in the morning, and five in the evening. Each cycle consisted of two weeks of medication, and one week without. In total, he had to complete eight cycles. He would soon experience side effects like joint aches, bloatedness, and hair loss.
26 June	Experienced an acute tummy ache that did not go away even after consulting a general practitioner.

28 June	Urgent review at the clinic on the same day after contacting the surgical team. After a series of scans and blood tests, he was diagnosed with intestinal obstruction secondary to adhesions, a known risk for anyone who has had a previous abdominal operation. The surgical team immediately arranged for admission and an emergency procedure. He was wheeled into the operating theatre that evening. After a two-hour procedure, the surgical team managed to relieve the blockage without the need for any resection of intestine.
7 July	After seven days in the hospital enduring liquid diet and the usual post-surgery discomfort, James was discharged. His previous experience with surgery had made him more adjusted to the recovery process this time round.
18 July	Two weeks after his discharge, James was able to begin his fifth cycle of chemotherapy where he would increase his dosage to 11 pills a day, up from 10.
28 August	After positive blood test readings, James was advised to increase his xeloda pill dosage to 12, six in the morning and six in the evening for his sixth chemotherapy cycle. This would be his final push towards recovery.
18 September–October	The duration of the seventh to eighth cycles was the hardest for James as he experienced the full side effects from his increased pill dosage. Aside from bloatedness, hair loss, and skin discoloration, he started to experience tenderness in his finger and feet joints, as well as peeling of his skin.
16 October	After completing his eighth and final chemotherapy cycle, scans indicated that there were no signs of cancer cells detected. He would still have to report for blood tests at regular intervals over the next five years to monitor his situation.

Message from Singapore Cancer Society

Over the past 60 years, SCS has relentlessly led the fight against cancer, providing an integrated continuum of care from cancer control and prevention, to patient support services, to survivorship and palliative care. Our key programmes and services include cancer screening programmes, public education, financial and welfare services, psychosocial support, survivorship, rehabilitation programmes, and hospice care. Like James' brave fight against cancer, you too, can come alongside SCS to support the cancer community to "Minimise Cancer and Maximise Lives". Further details on the Singapore Cancer Society can be found on *www.singaporecancersociety.org.sg*.

Albert Ching
Chief Executive Officer, Singapore Cancer Society

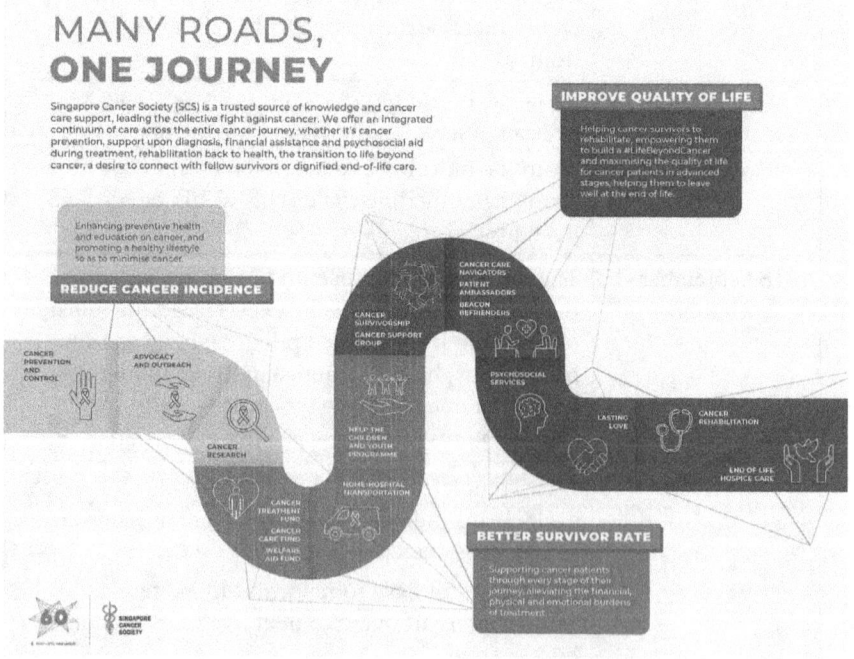

Acknowledgements

When I wrote *Running on Empty* back in 2017, I did wonder if James Wong would one day be willing to tell his fascinating story. I was certainly flattered when he first approached me for a discussion and even more so when he asked me to take on the project as author. I especially enjoyed his candid way of detailing his life experiences and welcomed the opportunity to peek into the insights and mindset of an elite athlete.

To prepare for the project, he started to journal his own experiences, feelings, high points, and setbacks in his battle with cancer. These entries proved vital not just in helping me piece together the events, but also in opening a window into his state of mind, which laid bare his strong determination to overcome his challenges, as well as his doubts and fears.

He was a product of a humble working-class family and had been brought up to believe that the patriarch of the family always had to demonstrate stoicism in the face of adversity. The vulnerabilities he had shared with me over the course of working on the project was a side of him I had never witnessed since I first got to know him 20 years ago. Who would've thought that the athlete who routinely struck fear into the hearts of his regional rivals suffered from anxiety as well! This was a fascinating insight which in turn made the project so much more meaningful. I thank James for entrusting me with his story and allowing me to exercise my own creative vision to tell it.

The rest of the Wong clan, Jana, Jessica, and Jordan were most accommodating with my frequent visits to their home. While they not only engaged me in lively conversations about what they went through as caregivers, but they also welcomed me with all manner of snack delights and an endless supply of tea. It always made my visits to their home such a pleasant experience.

Dr. Adrian Chiow, James' surgeon, kindly lent his professional services to proof-read the earlier drafts to help maintain medical authenticity to the story. He has also supported the project with a message of hope to cancer patients going through the same ordeal as James.

When it comes to my writing projects, I am always glad to be able to count on the advice and support of my mentor Chua Chong Jin. A former journalist with *The Straits Times*, Chong Jin had given me my first start in writing with short pieces for Team Singapore, Asian Athletics, and the former IAAF.[9] While I never really followed in his journalistic footsteps, his mentorship and advice through the years kept my flame for writing burning. Chong Jin contributed immensely to my previous project *Running on Empty*, and his ideas, suggestions, and input were once again invaluable after reading the early drafts to

---

[9] Now known as World Athletics or WA.

help me frame a suitable direction for this project and sharpen my ideas.

To trace James' career highs and lows, I relied heavily on the digital newspaper archives that resided within the National Library Board servers. His story was in a way pieced together by the tireless work of sports journalists across the years who had provided a clear public record of his sporting journey.

For results and statistics, other than online sources, I could call upon Singapore Athletics' High Performance Manager Mohamad Shahruddin who was most helpful in providing SEA Games results from the pre-2000 era where digital documentation was not always easily available.

For the images that brought the words to life, I relied on support from SportSG, the Singapore National Olympic Council, Singapore Athletics, as well as the personal archives of Ghana Segaran, Peh Siong San, and James himself.

I also thank the publishing team at World Scientific for helping me bring this story to print. The utmost professionalism demonstrated by the team not only helped me with my blind spots, but also refined the rough edges to my writing.

Finally, I'm grateful for my partner-in-crime Asmah who convinced me I had it in me for one more book, and then demonstrated the patience to sit through another project with me. I would not have embarked on this project without her love, support, and blessing.

Kenneth Khoo

Photo Credits

The publisher acknowledges the following for their kind permission to reproduce photos in this book:

- Personal archives of James Wong
  - p. 2
  - p. 9
  - p. 11
  - p. 13
  - p. 15
  - p. 17
  - p. 19
  - p. 22
  - p. 26
  - p. 30
  - p. 31
  - p. 32
  - p. 45
  - p. 48
  - p. 50
  - p. 53
  - p. 57
  - p. 58
  - p. 59
  - p. 62
  - p. 65
  - p. 66
  - p. 71
  - p. 72
  - p. 77
  - p. 79
  - p. 86
  - p. 95
  - p. 98
  - p. 106
  - p. 107
  - p. 108
  - p. 111
  - pp. 116–117
  - p. 127
  - p. 141
  - p. 149
  - p. 155
  - p. 167
  - p. 172
  - p. 177
  - p. 192
  - p. 200
  - p. 214
  - p. 218
  - p. 220
  - p. 229
  - p. 240
  - p. 242

Photo Credits

- Archives of Sport Singapore
  p. 166
  p. 179
  p. 181
  p. 183
  pp. 210–211

- Archives of Singapore National Olympic Council
  p. 102
  p. 130
  p. 132
  pp. 134–135
  p. 175

- Archives of Singapore Athletics
  p. 131
  pp. 188–189
  p. 205
  p. 219
  p. 222
  p. 223
  pp. 226–227

- Archives of Singapore Amateur Athletics Association
  p. 80
  p. 83

- Personal archives of Peh Siong San
  p. 146
  p. 169
  p. 170
  p. 174

- Personal archives of Ghana Segaran
  p. 230
  p. 232

About the Author

Kenneth Khoo was a former captain of the Singapore athletics team who had competed in the SEA Games from 2003 to 2015, winning a bronze medal in the 4x400m sprint relay in 2011.

Telling inspirational stories of athletes is his personal hobby and he has contributed articles about athletes and their stories to a number of online media and print publications.

In 2017, he took his dream one step further when he wrote *Running on Empty: The Story Behind 0.01s*, a biography of Singapore's former fastest man UK Shyam which was published by Ethos Books.

www.ingramcontent.com/pod-product-compliance
Lightning Source LLC
Chambersburg PA
CBHW061935220426
43662CB00012B/1918